Rural Catalonia under the Franco regime

Rural Catalonia under the Franco regime

THE FATE OF REGIONAL CULTURE
SINCE THE SPANISH CIVIL WAR

EDWARD C. HANSEN

Associate Professor and Chairman, Department of Anthropology
Queens College, City University of New York

CAMBRIDGE UNIVERSITY PRESS
CAMBRIDGE
LONDON · NEW YORK · MELBOURNE

Published by the Syndics of the Cambridge University Press
The Pitt Building, Trumpington Street, Cambridge CB2 1RP
Bentley House, 200 Euston Road, London NW1 2DB
32 East 57th Street, New York, NY 10022, USA
296 Beaconsfield Parade, Middle Park, Melbourne 3206, Australia

First published 1977

Printed in the United States of America

Typeset by David E. Seham Associates, Inc., Metuchen, New Jersey
Printed and bound by The Murray Printing Co., Westford, Massachusetts

Library of Congress Cataloging in Publication Data
Hansen, Edward C
Rural Catalonia under the Franco regime.
Bibliography: p.
1. Catalonia – Rural conditions.   2. Spain – Politics and government – 1939–
3. National characteristics, Catalonian.   4. Power (Social sciences)   I. Title.
HN590.C37H36 1977   309.1'46'7082   76–9177
ISBN 0 521 21457 2

CONTENTS

PREFACE

This work is an attempt to assess the impact of a modernizing authoritarian regime on a region traditionally hostile to the central government. Specifically, it is concerned with some of the effects of the Franco regime on Catalonian regional culture, as I observed them in one part of rural Catalonia during the 1960s. Central to this study is a concern with the nature of power, as it is developed and wielded on many different levels, and how power can be related to historical contradictions in regional and national society. The study of power in rural Catalonia has led to the analysis of complicated dialectical processes that seem to be operating all down the line, from the great institutions of government to individuals I knew in the field.

One of the motives for undertaking this work was to provide some information about what has been happening in Catalonia since the Franco regime took power in 1939 and imposed a virtual news blackout on developments in that region – testimony to the continuing sensitivity of the "Catalan question." Various concerned Catalans, who clearly must remain anonymous, spoke to me of the importance of conducting scholarly research into the transformations taking place in the region. The public dissemination of such research (even though anthropological research is necessarily small scale) would, they believed, bear on a vital national issue, if only because it would pump new information into an old political debate. The Catalans could not undertake such work themselves because of their own precarious political condition: Undertaking such a study, let alone attempting to publish the results, would likely lead to their imprisonment or exile. In their view a foreign researcher had a much better chance of surviving the political climate.

When I concluded my research in 1969, I submitted an outline of the work to Barral Editores in Barcelona, who accepted it with enthusiasm. I sent them a completed manuscript in the summer of 1972. Despite Barral's courageous efforts, the manuscript is still locked up in the Office of Censorship, Ministry of Tourism, within whose confines it has become widely read. Although I am gratified to have induced a measure of paranoia among some illustrious officials of the Spanish state, I had hoped for a wider audience and therefore decided to revise and update the work and publish it in English. After all, the relationship of fascism to people's lives in the developed world has again acquired immediacy.

This essay is not primarily an analysis of the operations of macrostructures (e.g., government, the economy) in rural Catalonia. The work springs from anthropological field research, and one of the cardinal missions of such research is to analyze the quality of life of actual people as they are observed working, making friends, marrying, and so forth. To this end, I spent twenty months between 1965 and 1969 in the Alto Panadés district of the province of Barcelona, generally observing the rhythms of life and change in a vinicultural district famous for the manufacture of champagne. Here, like most anthropologists, I spent most of my time trying to make my life intersect in as many ways as possible with those of the people who live in the various villages and towns. My wanderings led me across the fields of sharecroppers, through the mountains to coastal resort cities, into the bustling bars of Vilafranca (the county seat), through factories and government offices, and most importantly, into the homes of scores of magnificent and generous Catalans. I can only hope that my observations accurately reflect their conditions of life and thus in some small way repay their confidence in me.

The central concern of this work is to relate the facts of power to the lives of people and their culture. The principal focus is on power and its relationship to cultural institutions viewed, not as abstractions, but as *observable sets of social relations*. Although I have had to borrow from the more abstract works of political scientists and economists to construct a framework for my data, my task is to give life to these abstract considerations. That life I found on the streets and in the fields of the Alto Panadés. It is important to realize that in Catalonia in the 1960s, and today as well, much of local life was devoted to a studied evasion (not always successful) of institutional constructs of all sorts. It was lived informally, without charter, and in the absence of (sometimes in the face of) bureaucratic organization. The process of agrarian modernization, for example, cannot be understood without reference to friendships and patron-client relationships forged in the principal bars of Vilafranca. The observation and analysis of these small-scale coalitions are unique contributions of anthropology to the study of social change.

This book is not an isolated monograph about one more community in a remote rural area of the world. Rather, it is one contribution to a growing body of literature on the fates of regional cultures in the Mediterranean after World War II. Social scientists have recently begun to take an interest in the regionalism that has long been a principal concern of Mediterranean statesmen and citizens alike. This is in contrast to past anthropological practice, which emphasized the collection and codification of the oddments of regional cultures. The postwar integrative drives of many Mediterranean countries threaten to absorb regions into national bodies politic, rendering asunder the colorful fabrics of these cultures as they do so. My work was part of a series of field researches designed to investigate this process around the Mediterranean in the 1960s and coordinated by the departments of anthropology of the University of Michigan and University of Kent at Canterbury.

Many people have had a hand in the making of this book; their kindness I cannot thank enough. First and foremost I thank collectively the people of the Alto Panadés and hope they find this work a worthy account of their lives and times. For precautionary reasons, none of them can be mentioned by name. Furthermore, no identifiable people appear in the book; personality portraits are composite, and every effort has been made to protect the identities of friends and/or informants. The behavior described is real enough, and so is the district. The Alto Panadés is identified for two reasons: first, because the authorities knew well where I (and every other social scientist) was working in Spain; and second, because I wish to honor the hopes my friends expressed of having a book about their area. The traditional anthropological use of a pseudonym has not been resorted to here.

A number of other people have helped me both in the field and at home, frequently in decisive fashion. Foremost among them was Eric Wolf, who got me started and helped see me through as teacher, friend, and good man. Mervyn and Joan Meggitt supplied much advice on how fieldwork is done and provided me with many hours of fine companionship as well. Angel Palerm steered me to the right people in the field and shared with me his immense insights about Catalonia. Michael Kenny provided generous and intelligent counsel, both in Washington and in Madrid. Harry, Leona, and Kathlyn Tierney gave me friendship and a home away from home in the field and in London. Many members of the City University of New York's Mediterranean Research Group took time to read and criticize part or all of the manuscript. Among them were Pete and Jane Schneider, Ron Waterbury, Sydel Silverman, Ernestine Friedl, Bob Paul, Twig Johnson, Joe Aceves, Roger Sanjek, and Jeremy Beckett. Mollie Lamster typed much of the manuscript. Dorothy Obre is to be thanked for copyediting. With all this help, the book ought to be perfect: That it is not reflects on me alone.

This study would not have been possible without the financial support of various institutions. Foreign Area Fellowship Program provided basic support for 1965–6, and generously allotted me a dissertation write-up grant for 1967. The National Science Foundation awarded me a supplemental grant for 1965–6 that enabled me to purchase much-needed field equipment. The University of Michigan Mediterranean Area Project subsidized my fieldwork in May–June 1967. Summer fieldwork in 1969 was done under a CUNY Research Foundation Grant. This grant provided sufficient funds for me to hire a research assistant, Jerry A. Jacobs, then an undergraduate at Queens, to whom I am thankful for research help.

Finally, perhaps the greatest debt of all I owe to my wife, Elizabeth de G. R. Hansen, who has worked with me steadily on this book and endured all my exasperating idiosyncrasies. It is to her that I dedicate this book.

E. C. H.

Carmel, New York
August 1975

1

A government, a region, and the Alto Panadés: introduction

The principal goal of this work is to trace the fate of rural Catalonian culture under the modernization program instituted by the Franco regime (1939–75) and, so far, continued by the government of King Juan Carlos. Catalonia, with its distinctive language and culture, has been for centuries a major obstacle to the political integration of the Spanish nation. As the economic mainstay and political bellwether of the ill-starred Spanish Republic (1931–9), Catalonia is still viewed today as a hostile region by the central government. Since the end of the Spanish civil war in 1939, the Catalans suffered a systematic and thorough repression at the hands of the Franco regime. The repression, coupled with the regime's version of national modernization, eroded much of the fabric of Catalan social life, negating nearly nine centuries of regional development. Part of the mission of this study is to record the vibrancy of regional institutions before they pass into history, victims of the expansion of state power in the twentieth century.

So often when anthropologists write about cultural demise, we are but sad witnesses to the seemingly inexorable workings of evolution: A primitive or peasant society is overwhelmed by the encroachment of a more economically and politically developed society. At best, our studies underline the humanity of the victims and embody a plea for compassion for and empathy with the doomed peoples of the earth. At first glance, the fate of Catalonia appears to be one more episode in the already voluminous literature of cultural decline. As but one region of a rapidly modernizing country, burdened with a culture redolent of feudal symbolism, Catalonia might appear a logical candidate for cultural extinction.

But such is not the case. Far from being a backward region in a developing nation, Catalonia had become by the end of the nineteenth century the only region in Spain to generate an industrial revolution. Spearheaded by an aggressive indigenous bour-

1

geoisie, this industrial revolution appeared to be on the verge of spreading throughout the nation by the onset of the twentieth century. For a time, it seemed that Spain would take its place among European nations as a modern industrial country. The role of the Catalan bourgeoisie in national development would closely parallel that of the other European bourgeoisie that had preceded it.

Yet the very industrial revolution it had ushered in led the Catalan bourgeoisie first into bitter conflict with the Spanish state and ultimately into a social revolution within Catalonia. The failure of the Catalan bourgeoisie was a political failure triggered by its economic successes. At the heart of this political failure was the inability of the Catalan industrialists to dominate the apparatus of the Spanish state, to which the less developed regions of the country had long-established prior claims. Without the power of the state behind it, the bourgeoisie was able neither to dominate Spain economically nor to maintain hegemony over the popular classes in Catalonia. The political eclipse of the Catalan bourgeoisie was complete by the outbreak of the civil war in July 1936. Since that time it has increasingly become a political and economic dependent of the central government, without any developmental initiatives of its own.

A major concern of this study is to analyze the transformation of the Catalan bourgeoisie from a class that once aggressively pursued the goals of the autonomous national development to a docile dependent of an authoritarian regime. The regime has its own version of national development, which is the antithesis of the indigenous entrepreneurial growth advocated by the Catalan bourgeoisie. The government-advocated growth is predicated on increasingly close dependent ties with the already developed industrial economies of Europe and the United States. It increasingly stresses the importation of technology and capital from these centers, giving this kind of modernization a distinctly foreign cast. For Catalan businessmen modernization provides new opportunities to make money, but none to influence basic governmental decision making.

The conflict between Catalonia and the less developed regions of Spain was not merely a struggle among regional elites for the control of state power, but a more deeply rooted conflict between entire social orders. The Catalan bourgeoisie did not appear overnight to challenge the elites of the less developed regions of Spain;

it arose out of a centuries-long process of socioeconomic growth within Catalonia. This process of growth had created a distinctively Catalan social order, defined by characteristic regional institutions that organized people's lives in terms of work, play, and love, as well as politics. Thus an anthropological study of the fate of these institutions under the Franco regime and the present government cannot be concerned only with abstract developmental considerations; it must deal also with transformations of the quality of that life.

To accomplish these varied ends, I studied three Catalan cultural institutions during the course of anthropological field research in the Alto Panadés, a juridical district[1] in the province of Barcelona, prominent in both nineteenth-century development and subsequent modernization. These institutions are (1) the *rabassa morta* system of sharecropping, the juridical vehicle of nineteenth-century bourgeois economic expansion into the countryside and a prime source of class conflict in the district; (2) the cultural-recreational associations that served initially as public forums for bourgeois ideology and popular political mobilization and ultimately as the repositories of popular civic and political action; and (3) the *hereu-pubilla* marriage-inheritance system that until recently served both to protect family business holdings and to generalize a property ethic throughout Catalonia.

After three and a half decades of the Franco regime, these characteristic regional cultural institutions have lost much of their vitality and increasingly their viability as well. Within the brief span of their lifetimes, Catalans have witnessed their cultural decline. Although a few Catalans see prospects for self-fulfillment in the modernization, most are saddened and bewildered witnesses of this process. Even as regional culture is being laid to rest, the government has created a replacement in the form of entirely new socioeconomic opportunities. Yet the Catalans can seize these opportunities only by renouncing the society that nurtured them through their formative years. How culture dies and individuals rise in the process of modernization is a recurring theme of this book.

This work is organized as follows: The remainder of Chapter 1 provides a short discussion of the Spanish government and a brief sketch of the Alto Panadés. Chapter 2 traces the development of regional culture since the Middle Ages, stressing the evolution of the Catalan bourgeoisie. Chapters 3 to 5 are concerned with an analysis of the institutions selected for study in the Alto Panadés. Chapter 6 examines some of the more formal aspects of power in the Alto Panadés. Chapter 7 summarizes the impact of the central government on rural Catalonian culture. Connections between the Catalan experience and other areas of the underdeveloped world are suggested. Finally, for the more intrepid general reader and for colleagues interested in the technical aspects of this study, an appendix describing field procedures is provided.

The Franco regime: a paradigm of state power

Unifying the diverse goals of this study is a concern with the organization of power in Spain and specifically with how this power affects the lives of Catalans living in the Alto Panadés. No government ever had the corrosive impact on Catalan culture that the Franco regime had. We are today witnessing the dissolution of a culture that until now has managed to survive and flourish despite centuries of opposition from hostile governments, natural catastrophes, and endemic internal turmoil. Clearly the Franco government was nothing like the Castilian military governments that used to arise to restore public order and national morality (Payne 1967a:14–30 and passim). It was, rather, a fully modern government of a type increasingly common in the underdeveloped world and commonly described in the political science literature as a "modernizing authoritarian regime."

It is not my purpose here to reiterate the formal properties of authoritarian regimes so well presented elsewhere (e.g., Linz 1962; Payne 1967b; Erickson 1970; R. Schneider 1971; Schmitter 1971; R. Hansen 1971). Instead, this outline focuses on the ways the Franco government managed to wield effective power in Catalonia, where all preceding governments had failed. It supplies, not an analysis of the workings of complicated government machinery at national and local levels, but an explanation of the general power contexts in which Catalans now relate to the central government and vice versa. It should serve the reader as a guide to the remainder of the book, in which the workings of power are described simply as part of the daily life of people in the Alto Panadés.

The argument presented here has two main points, each involving different kinds and uses of power. First, much of the government's power in Catalonia derives from the fact that the government itself is now the most dynamic agent of economic change in the region and has displaced the Catalan bourgeoisie in this capacity. National modernization in Spain involves the penetration of foreign capital into the region, the allotment of state credits to a wide variety of enterprises, a proliferation of state agencies connected with credit and technical assistance programs, and the implementation of at least the rudiments of a consumer economy. Simultaneously, the government consistently blocks local developmental initiatives on the part of the Catalan bourgeoisie. It does, however, consistently provide means of incorporating certain bourgeois goals within its own programs and administrative structures (see Chapter 3 for an extended discussion of this point).

Here we are discussing power as a system of rewards and sanctions under the control of the national government. We can observe the workings of power at this level in Lasswell's terms of "who gets what, when, and how." It is worth emphasizing once more that critical resources in the Alto Panadés (e.g., arable land and capital) have had conflicting claims upon them for a very long time, so that the government's intervention is as potentially decisive in major social questions as in economic issues. It is equally worth noting that at present the key to economic modernization in rural Catalonia, as it is conceived by the regime, lies in the allocation of capital (in the form of credits), the provision of technical assistance, and the importation of agricultural machinery – all matters decided by the government alone.

To influence the allocation of resources is simultaneously to transform the social arrangements that underlay the former distribution of resources. What is interesting in the case of rural Catalonia is not the confirmation of this truism, but the manner in which this transformation is taking place. In spite of its relative political strength, the regime cannot promote its programs with dispatch, partly because it came to power after a revolution and presides over a society still bitterly divided, and partly because it lacks sufficient essential resources for rapid development, such as capital, trained personnel, and administrative density. Both these factors select for gradualism in the promotion of government programs, rather than for dramatic, rapid changes with their unsettling consequences.

The government's programs create a potential for change that offers the local bourgeoisie in the Alto Panadés very favorable possibilities if it can organize itself around these programs. As we will see in Chapters 5 and 6, it is not easy for the haute bourgeoisie to generate the necessary local organization to cash in on these opportunities. Yet so much time and effort are spent in organizing the minuscule coalitions necessary to the successful prosecution of agrarian modernization that a useful corollary definition of power is "the distribution of energy in a social system" (Schneider et al. 1972:334).

The second important point of my argument is that the government's drive toward national modernization depends on its ability to repress successfully all its political opponents, especially the popular classes of the nation, who have long been imbued with revolutionary visions of a new Spain. Under the Franco regime, the ubiquitous national police forces reached new levels of efficiency and the army an unprecedented level of loyalty to a single general (Payne 1967a,b). The government was world famous for the efficiency, organization, and vigor with which it repressed Spanish political life. Indeed, it was probably an inspiration to many similar regimes elsewhere in the third world, if for no other reason than its longevity. When power is discussed in this context, the Weberian concept of legitimate authority is rapidly discarded in favor of Lenin's (1952:206–8) view of the state as "special bodies of armed men." Let us examine each of these main points and their interrelationships.

Schneider et al. (1972:340) describe the kind of economic transformation that is taking place in Spain under the rubric of modernization[2] as a "process by which an underdeveloped region [or country] changes in response to inputs (ideologies, behavioral codes, commodities and institutional models) from already established industrial centers, a process which is based on that region's continued dependence upon the urban-industrial metropolis."

Though it is impossible to detail here the depth of penetration of foreign capital into Spain and its implications for the nation's economic growth,[3] it is useful to highlight those aspects that are relevant to the present Catalan experience. Most pertinent to this discussion is the fact that much of Spain's economic growth is increasingly dependent on foreign capital, which enters the country in at least three ways. The first way is direct foreign participation in, and often outright control of, the most technologically complex and capital-intensive enterprises in Spain. Commenting on the penetration of foreign firms in the areas of chemical and metallurgical industries, auto manufacturing, energy, and high finance, economist Ramón Tamames writes:

If the penetration of American capital and technology is being felt each year more strongly in the industrially advanced nations of the Common Market or the EFTA [European Free Trade Association], to the point where one already speaks, not without justification, of an American technological and capitalist domination over the old Continent – it is hardly strange that with a more reduced market and a more backwards technology, Spain is each year more penetrated by foreign capital. [1970:355–6]

Foreign capital is not confined, however, to capital-intensive or technologically complex enterprises; it has also entered increasingly into light industrial enterprises, where it is sometimes in direct competition with native entrepreneurs. Additionally, it has even penetrated into some critical areas of real estate (e.g., hotel construction), traditionally one of the economic bastions of Spanish capitalists of all regions (Tamames 1970:357).

A third major source of foreign capital, even more important than direct foreign investment, comes from the millions of tourists who visit Spain each year. By 1968, roughly 35 percent of the gross national income was derived from the visits of over 19 million tourists to Spain, and tourist dollars were providing the principal source of foreign exchange for the national treasury (Tamames 1970:335–9 and passim). Ironically, citizens of the democratic countries of Europe and the United States did more to underwrite the costs of the Franco regime with their vacation moneys than did foreign capitalists with all their investments.

Though the financial revenues derived from tourism obviously are at the heart of much of the government's economic dynamism, the social and economic spinoffs from tourism are very complex.[4] Tourism has created jobs for many Spaniards who otherwise might be unemployed because of the stagnancy in agriculture; construction trades are thriving, as hotels and restaurants continue to be built at a record pace. And in areas rich in tourism and with a declining peasantry, like the Mediterranean portions of Catalonia, part of the peasantry stands to be converted into the "army of waiters and soda pop vendors" that Carlos Fuentes (1969) spoke of in Cuernavaca, Mexico.

Tourism has also a social character, at least for those Spaniards who are in continuous contact with it: It provides them with a vision of what life is apparently like in the developed countries. Yet the image of life style projected by the tourist in Spain hardly mirrors the realities of, say, middle-class existence in Toledo, Ohio. Tourists often are tourists in order to escape temporarily from the cultural confinements of their own countries. Their apparent freedom of action, coupled with their affluence, provide an appeal based on a distorted perception of what the tourist's life is like in his own country. Tourism no doubt helps to stimulate demand for foreign goods in the nascent consumer economy (Schneider et al. 1972:343).

Although foreign sources of capital are critical to the Spanish economy, the regime also actively backs some of the efforts of domestic enterprises through extensive governmental programs of credits and expansion of governmental agencies for technical assistance (Tamames 1970). Of particular interest to this study are the ways in which state credits and technical assistance are provided to agricultural enterprises in rural Catalonia. As we shall see in Chapter 3, the state has progressively intervened in the agricultural economy of the Alto Panadés in everything from new decrees relating to land tenure to the financing of mechanization and the construction of a vinicultural cooperative. This intervention leaves little initiative to local entrepreneurial talents; the local bourgeoisie must follow the state's directives or come up empty-handed. The dependent status of the Catalan bourgeoisie all over the region is underlined by the fact that in this era of high finance, the Catalan enterpreneurial class does not have controlling interest in even one bank of national importance (Linz and Miguel 1966:274–5).

Having outlined the features of the Spanish economy most pertinent to this study, we now turn to more direct questions of power. Who is the political force behind the forging of this economy of dependency? How is power actually wielded through the apparatus of the state? In answering, we are aided by Juan Linz's essay on the authoritarian regime, in which he uses Spain as the archetype. According to Linz:

Authoritarian regimes are political systems with limited, not responsible, political pluralism, without elaborate and guiding ideology (but with distinctive mentalities); without intensive or extensive political mobilizations (except at some points in their development) and in which a leader (or occasionally a small group) exercises power within formally ill-defined limits, but actually quite predictable ones. [1962:297]

Standing at the apex of the governmental structure, in the positions of power and command as heads of ministries of the regime, has been a wide variety of men of the Old Spain. Linz's (1962:330 and passim) sociopolitical profiles of cabinet ministers since 1939 reveal that the ministries have been dominated by the various political components of the pre–civil war Spanish Right; representatives of the military, Monarchist, Falangist, and Catholic political groupings have held the lion's share of cabinet posts. Definitively excluded from the pinnacles of power are representatives of the Republican, Left, or regional Nationalist parties that advocated their versions of a new Spain before the Spanish civil war.[5] Not only are they excluded from power, but they have been the principal targets of governmental repression.

This cursory examination of who has held cabinet posts since the advent of the Franco regime suggests simple continuity of pre–civil war Spanish politics under a new guise. In this regime, as in so many of its predecessors, the elites have been recruited from central and southern Spain and are the very elites under whose aegis Spain declined so disastrously in the nineteenth century. Furthermore, these elites long encouraged foreign investment and national economic dependency on the industrialized nations of Europe (Carr 1966:265–70). Insofar as the present government is inclined in the same direction, it seems to be governed by them in accordance with their own interests.

Yet this position oversimplifies the power realities of the Franco regime. The government's main accomplishment, in which it differs from any of its predecessors, has been to expand radically the power of the state at the expense of all other interests, including to a large extent those of the parochial elites incorporated in it. Regional power domains spearheaded by these elites have largely been usurped by the expansion of state power, not only in Catalonia, but everywhere in the nation. The fragmentation of power into regional and even local domains characteristic of pre–civil war Spain was brought to an end by the Franco regime, which arrogated to itself an effective monopoly of political power. Coupled with an effective expansion of the means of force has been a growth of governmental intervention in the management of the national economy; only the state, as opposed to any elite, now has the technical and financial capacity to manage the country. Thus, though cabinet personnel are preponderantly drawn from the traditional elites and political groupings in Spain, they act not simply in their own interests, but as servants of a state with much more diffuse interests than their own.

To protect the dependent capitalist elites from the depredations of the popular classes, to encourage foreign investment, and to make sure tourists enjoy their visits to Iberia, the regime must be first and foremost the guarantor of national peace and tranquility. It is to achieve these ends that repression is so systematically prosecuted. But only part of the repression consists in the celebrated performance of the national political police forces. Of deeper importance are the attempts to depoliticize many Spaniards who have had a prior political education and a political life. In contrast to the situation earlier in this century, the only good citizen is an apathetic one. In fact, varying Linz's (1962) argument a little, it can be said that political apathy is now the highest civic virtue in Spain.

Whatever conflicts cannot be overcome by force, propaganda, and material inducements are channeled into the structure of the regime itself. Thus, for example, the Spanish working class and, to a lesser extent, the various Spanish peasantries are now integrated with the Spanish capitalists into vertical syndicates, with state labor bureaucrats as the ultimate arbiters of disputes between these two classes. Such unnatural marriages inevitably have some stormy consequences. Though these intramural conflicts can be observed in the workings of the syndicates, they are perhaps more colorful in the church, one of the official paragons of the regime. As we shall see in Chapter 6, the divisions between the lower clergy and the hierarchy have come to represent the old class struggle, albeit with a theological tinge to its ideological component. Suffice it to say that there can be no popular participation in politics under the present Spanish government.

How does this organization of power in the central government affect the Catalans? This question is the reason for writing the book, and several major points can be previewed at this point. First, the Catalan bourgeoisie, though it benefits materially from the government, has neither representation nor initiatives in the regime. Far from being an independent aggressive bourgeoisie interested in independent national (or even regional) development, it is now as much a dependence elite as its Castilian counterpart. Second, Catalonian culture is being destroyed by the regime's repression and modernization policies, and a new kind of culture is taking its place. This new culture is a culture of modernization, including rampant consumerism and proletarianization of the popular classes. From the popular Catalan perspective, the regime, as Linz (1970) points out, is only a state, which imposes its will by force on a politically impotent people. It does not give the Catalans a sense of nationhood, in the way Ortega y Gasset (1937:16–7) meant when he described a "nation" as "a project which suggests collective life" in which people "do not live to be together . . . but to do something together."

The Alto Panadés: the land and the people

Physical features

The Alto Panadés is one of many mountain valleys that make up the Mediterranean prelittoral depression. Though the district itself is landlocked, its eastern reaches are but a few kilometers from the sea, and it lies roughly halfway between the Catalan port cities of Barcelona and Tarragona. The valley is trough-shaped, running approximately 27 kilometers southwest by northeast, and 22 kilometers due east and west. The sides of the trough are made up of several related but distinct low mountain ranges, which reach as high as 1,000 meters above sea level but are generally at altitudes ranging from 100 to 300 meters above sea level. Within the floor of the trough, the terrain is far from level, and rapid changes of topography regularly occur every several hundred meters. The principal geographic and demographic features are portrayed in the accompanying map. Radiating outward from Vilafranca del Panadés, the principal city of the *comarca* (region), is a network of roads that integrates the district internally and connects it with the major population centers of Catalonia. Thus Vilafranca is linked to both Valencia and Barcelona by a national highway, and to the small industrial city of Igualada and the major resort town of Sitges by a major provincial road. Wending their way outward from Vilafranca are various tortuous provincial roads that connect the city with twenty villages and numerous hamlets that make up the agrarian component of the *comarca*. The road system underlies an essential feature of the Alto Panadés – its openness toward the world

Map 1.   *Catalonia in Spain*

Map 2.   *The Comarca Panadés in Catalonia*

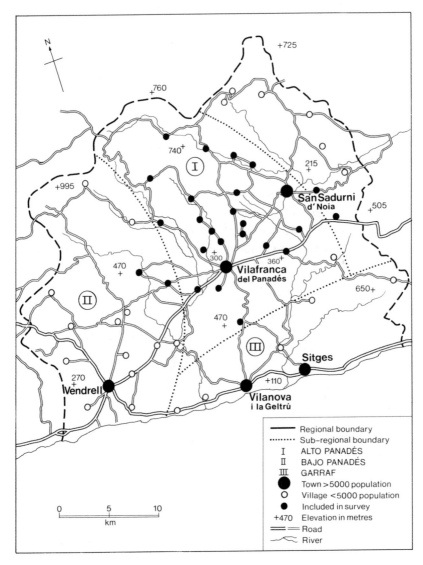

Map 3. *The Comarca Panadés and its divisions*

outside its boundaries. For centuries, the valley has been an important transportation and communications link between major Catalonian cities. In Roman times, Vilafranca was a garrison town on the Via Augusta; today the same road bears a heavy volume of truck and tourist traffic from Barcelona to Valencia. The constant throbbing of overloaded lorries along the main street of Vilafranca, the clouds of dust rising off the road, and the stench of diesel exhaust fumes remind one that Vilafranca is thoroughly familiar with all that is modern. A scant 30 miles from Barcelona, Vilafranca has always been drawn into the great socioeconomic convulsions of Catalonia's metropolis. In brief, the Alto Panadés is no remote agrarian district with minimal contact with the outside world; rather, it is a ready recipient of all forces for social change because of its intense contacts with thriving metropolitan centers.

Although Vilafranca owes much of its reputation in Catalonia to its strategic geographic position within the region, the Alto Panadés derives its principal fame as a viti- and vinicultural region. The peculiar soil and climatic conditions of the region combine to allow the cultivation of the most productive vineyards in Catalonia. At harvest time, the grapes are so thick on the suckers that they begin to force the vines, some nearly as thick as pier stanchions, to the ground. Whereas the vines of the neighboring Bajo Panadés generally yield between 2 and 3 kilos each, those of the Alto Panadés produce 8 to 10 kilos (Giró 1966:6). It is not the productivity of the vines alone that makes the *comarca* a relatively prosperous vinicultural area, but that the grapes can be converted into champagne. The Alto Panadés is *the* champagne district of Spain, a fact that sets it apart from the many districts that can only produce table wines.

A glance at the countryside that generates this champagne industry reveals the dominance of vineyards over all other forms of cultivation. Vine is present everywhere, spreading from the fertile valley floor up the barren slopes of the mountains that ring the district. The cultivation of vineyards on such difficult slopes reflects the overexpansion of this crop during the nineteenth century, when the wine market was much better than it is today. Each year now brings a further retrenchment of viticulture and its increasing concentration on the valley floor. Concomitantly, vineyards on the slopes are being abandoned, and there are even two mountain villages now without inhabitants.

In the vast majority of the arable land of the Alto Panadés, cultivation of vineyards is still the principal economic activity. Yet the techniques of farming as well as the size and quality of holdings are far from homogeneous. There are over 5,000 agricultural properties here, ranging from less than 1 hectare to more than 1,000 hectares (Giró 1966:3). The fragmented nature of property holdings combines with the ruggedness of the terrain to produce a crazy-quilt pattern in agricultural properties. It is not unusual to see within a few square hectares the small holdings of four or five different landholders, each growing a distinct crop on his plot. Perhaps the most typical arrangement is vineyards interspersed with fields of wheat, the latter being the traditional fallow crop for vine.

No arable land is wasted in this complex web of small and medium-sized properties. Small stretches of land bordering on seasonal rivers are generally put to use as vegetable gardens, which can be sown two or three times a year, each time with different crops. Between many of the fields are olive trees, which afford their owners a small annual earning while simultaneously serving as boundary markers. Here and there, a farmer has ripped up a vineyard and planted a peach or apple orchard in its stead, hoping these fruits will be more remunerative than grapes. Even less frequently, an enterprising cultivator has installed some form of irrigation system for a small garden, in an effort to circumvent the lack of water the district has long suffered from. In sum, the countryside of the Alto Panadés, though dominated by viticulture, yields a wide variety of agricultural produce, cultivated under diverse natural conditions.

The cultivation of arable land is so extensive that there is scarcely room for livestock; yet almost all rural families manage to maintain a few animals, if only in the courtyards of their own homes. Both pastureland and forest were nearly eliminated by the spread of viticulture in the nineteenth century; yet the need for both animals and fuel grew as vineyard and population expanded. To meet these needs, Catalan farmers have adopted some ingenious methods. Few rural homes lack penned animals, typically chickens and rabbits for home consumption and for sale in the weekly village markets. Since much of the work in vineyards requires the use of horses as draft animals, a horse is often quartered in the first floor of a peasant's house, in a stable adjacent to the kitchen. In addition

Catalonian polyculture

to providing the energy for cultivation, the horse also provides valuable fertilizer for the crops.[6]

The relationship between man and land is even more elaborate if we consider the farmer's utilization of things he does not cultivate or of things that are by-products of his efforts. In the slopelands, where few people farm any longer, a peasant can find all manner of herbs that both season his food and supply his medicine chest. In addition to the herbs that convert simple subsistence foods such as artichokes and potatoes into sumptuous feasts, the vineyards and surrounding mountains produce other regional delicacies, including a variety of snails and a pinkish pungent mushroom typically broiled with minced garlic.

The vine itself has had to substitute for the forest it largely replaced in the past two centuries. Dried suckers for kindling and dead vines used as logs are the principal sources of heat and cooking fire for the rural residents of the Alto Panadés. Only recently has butane gas (in portable cylinders) begun to supplant vine as the main source of heat in the district. Yet even with the ready availability of gas, its cost (and the cost of related appliances such as stoves and water heaters) necessitates continued reliance on vine, so that most rural residents still suffer from cold and lack of hot water in the winter.

The countryside of the Alto Panadés is not only highly productive, but very beautiful. Its uneven terrain provides dramatic and sudden shifts of landscapes, each one seemingly more spectacular than the last. Among the magnificent views the district offers is that of the mountain of Montserrat, the spiritual center of Catalonia.[7] What greatly enhances the natural beauty of the Alto Panadés is the way sunlight filters through the skies over the Mediterranean. The intensity of this light sharpens all the images the landscapes create: In an enormous vineyard, each vine seems to be perfectly outlined, and the color and architectural detail of houses on faraway slopes stand out in bold relief. At midday, the sunlight becomes so intense that the extremes of color converge on a shimmering and nearly spectral white, as though the sun had bleached everything it touched. Then as late afternoon approaches, the spectrum of colors reemerges, with each color enhanced by a subtle golden overtone.

Spread out among these splendid rural scenes are the villages and hamlets that house most of the district's peasantry. The twenty-three villages average about 1,000 people each and usually appear as compact settlements nestled among the vineyards. The houses of country people are generally solid, large constructions of rough concrete; some people have attempted to decorate their dwellings by capping the concrete with a coat of Portland cement and then whitewashing it. These constructions reflect the lack of wood in the Alto Panadés; only the ceiling beams and doors of the houses are wooden. The size of most of the houses reflects both the larger families of an earlier era and the continued visits of relatives who no longer live in the villages.

Not all the agriculturalists live in the villages. Many dwell in small clusters of houses that adjoin the fields they work. Frequently, these hamlets are located near a great estate *(masia)* and house the estate's sharecropping families. *Masias* are enormous dwellings whose squat bulk and somber colors make them resemble fortresses. These are the homes of the rich people of the Alto Panadés, but few are elegant, although most have a quiet dignity. The fancier *masias* have formal gardens replete with fountains and, on occasion, a private chapel where mass was once said for the exclusive benefit of the members of the household. Frequently, the *masia* grounds also house a winery, where the fruits delivered by sharecroppers at harvest time are converted into champagnes and table wines.

The countryside of the Alto Panadés gives a deceptive impression of somnolence and tradition, of agriculture carried on in the same fashion as in the past century. Most fields are tilled by a man with a horse and plow; much wine is still made in sharecroppers' homes; even the *masias* seem to belong to an earlier time. But right alongside the farmer trudging behind his horsedrawn plow is someone else cultivating his field with a tractor. And not all the *masias* house feisty old rentier capitalists, struggling to maintain a leisurely pace of existence; some are home to energetic businessmen who are purchasing farm machinery to experiment with new crops and agricultural techniques.

Modernization in the countryside can be seen in much more than tractors and experimental plots. Just a few kilometers from Vilafranca along the highway to Barcelona stands a vinicultural cooperative, built in 1966 with funds provided by the state. Complete with the latest equipment for the conversion of grapes into quality wines, it will considerably improve those wines that have heretofore been processed under the floor of the sharecroppers' stables. The cooperative includes not only sharecroppers, but various large farmers as well. A partnership between some of these men and pertinent government officials led to the founding of the cooperative in the first place and illustrates the dynamic intervention of the state in the district's economy. And modernization is not confined to agriculture; in fact some aspects of the former are antithetical to the latter. Since 1960 some prize vineyards near the Barcelona-Tarragona highway have been ripped up to make room for new factories. This process accelerates each year, as Barcelona's industry long ago surpassed its geographic limits. Logically, the spillover from the metropolis follows the main highways, promising that Vilafranca will undergo industrial growth for many years to come. Characteristically, this is light industry: New plants installed along the highway manufacture chicken feed, fertilizer, cement, bras and girdles, and shoe polish, to cite typical examples. These facilities are not all generated by Catalan capital; German, Italian, and American interests have established themselves in the Alto Panadés in the past fifteen years, with more of their compatriots doubtless to follow.

New agricultural techniques and factories are not the whole process of modernization in the *comarca*. The upsurge of industry and the boom in tourism have created a new market for diverse types of real estate in the Alto Panadés. For instance, as the decline in demand for wine has led to a contraction of viticulture away from the more mountainous lands of the district, this same land has suddenly become valuable for the construction of vacation home developments for middle-class city dwellers who cannot afford such a spot on the coast. Similarly, a number of fancy restaurants are appearing in particularly scenic spots in the countryside, hoping to cater to both foreign tourists and Catalan summer residents. Should the tourist boom continue to grow as it has so spectacularly since 1960, the Alto Panadés will undergo a much greater expansion of such facilities with an even greater reduction of agricultural land as one result.

Modernization affects the life styles of rural people in many other ways. Most readily observable is the impact of consumerism, which has penetrated every household in the Alto Panadés to some degree. Few homes lack a radio, and a growing number have television. Thus each family is now bombarded with the advertisements so familiar to the citizens of developed capitalist countries. These stimuli have their effects, particularly on the young, who rush to purchase readymade clothes, motor bikes, watches, and the like. But the articles for consumption are less important than the cumulative orientation of consumerism itself. Consumerism provides a distinct alternative to orienting one's life toward the acquisition of land, a goal widespread among country youth until a few years ago. Instead of the traditional saving and reinvesting habits of the Catalan peasant, consumerism offers the peasant youth instant escape from the drudgery of agriculture and more intimate contact with metropolitan life styles. Consumerism can be seen as one way of smoothing the transition from peasant to proletarian.

The rapid rhythm of life in Vilafranca del Panadés provides a marked contrast with that of the surrounding countryside. In this former medieval garrison town some 15,000 people are jammed into grayish-orange-plastered apartment buildings and private homes, some with central heating and even elevators, but most with dark, winding staircases and few modern conveniences. People are lucky to find space to live in; the recent rush of industry and concomitant labor migration into the district have left Vilafranca short of homes for about 5,000 people (Anon. 1966:10), forcing many working-class people to find lodging in nearby villages. The stacking of person upon person, house upon house, is relieved intermittently by small squares or plazas. As many of the squares are new, there has not yet been time to pave them or plant grass in them, although energetic city officials are working hard to do so. In the newer sections of town, usually working-class neighborhoods, the plaza is apt to consist of a plot of dusty earth, raised 1 or 2 meters above street level, and advertising a drinking fountain as its principal ornament.

In spite of the housing problems brought about by rapid population growth, Vilafranca manages to conserve much of the physical splendor of its feudal past. In the heart of the city, for example, in the Plaza Pio XII, stand a fourteenth-century palace and a twelfth-century basilica side by side. Facing them across the plaza is an enormous thirteenth-century house where, it is rumored, King Pere II of Catalonia died centuries ago. But not all of this square is a tribute to the architecture of the Middle Ages; in its center stands a monument to *els castellers* that celebrates the traditional Catalan sport of erecting human towers.[8] The square commemorates the regionalist spirit as well as the feudal past.

As the Plaza Pio XII provides the town with a sense of history, the two major tree-lined promenades *(ramblas)*, typical of Catalan cities, serve Vilafranca as focal points of commerce and public intercourse. Along these gracious thoroughfares are located many of the town's 600 businesses, the three major social clubs, and the fancier public bars. The *ramblas* lend order to the anarchic public life of the *comarca* by giving Catalan cities a geographic sense of social and economic concentration. In a region with such a diffuse economy and fragmented social activity, the importance of this concentration in explaining the coherence of Catalan society cannot be underestimated.

Inhabitants

To this point, we have been concerned with the physical description of the Alto Panadés. However, the principal concern of this work is with the people who live in this area of Catalonia. As we are dealing with some 45,000 people spread out in twenty-three villages and two towns, it is imperative to classify them in some way that will make their study manageable. Because much of this work is an exercise in political economy, the most useful way to classify local people is in terms of social class. I have grouped the region's inhabitants according to the ways they relate to the means of production, that is, according to their differential access to strategic resources (Stavenhagen 1967). Though this sort of classification is objective because it is culture-free,[9] it is not simply an arbitrary classification imposed by a foreign social scientist. Catalonia has a rich history of class conflict, and despite the modernization of recent years, class boundaries have not undergone the "blurring" or "decomposition" described by Dahrendorf (1959) for advanced industrial societies. Local citizens have a highly developed sense of class position and their vocabulary is frequently tinged with overtones of political economy, a reflection of the recent political discord in the area.

All that need concern us here is the allocation of land, labor, and capital in the *comarca*. In Chapter 3 a more precise accounting of their distribution is offered in conjunction with the description of the evolution of class relations in the area. Because local statistical indexes of property (e.g., land surveys and tax records) are not recorded on the basis of social class, it has been necesary to extrapolate class data from these records. Consequently, the number of people in each class is an approximation, just as is this outline of the distribution of property in the Alto Panadés. It is easiest to consider the population in terms of families, instead of individuals, because property statistics and tax records list only heads of household and because many inhabitants of the district are children and therefore not part of the active economic population.

At the apex of the class structure stand roughly 250 families who can be classified as the local representatives of the haute bourgeoisie. The head of each of these families owns at least one substantial tract of agricultural property, a minimum of 20 hectares and a maximum of 1,000 hectares. Additionally, he possesses at least one light industrial establishment, frequently a winery, and several rental properties in addition to the family home or homes. This class forms the economic linchpin of the *comarcal* economy because it holds both the bulk of productive property and the lion's share of available capital. Having initiated the nineteenth-century recolonization of the district, these families are now the primary beneficiaries of the Franco regime's modernization drive.

Beneath the haute bourgeoisie stand the 1,200 families of the local petite bourgeoisie, of which half live in Vilafranca and the remainder are dispersed throughout the countryside. These families generally make the bulk of their living from small family businesses, frequently no more than a one-room store. The limited scope of their enterprises can be inferred from the fact that less than 15 percent of their businesses hire anyone outside the family. In addition to their small businesses, these families possess small vineyards, usually several hectares. Members of this class frequently have one modest rental property that supplements their small but comfortable incomes. Many also raise a few chickens and/or rabbits in their courtyards, even in Vilafranca, reaffirming their sharecropper origins. This class best represents the level of popular aspiration in rural Catalonia: a secure income derived from a handful of modestly prosperous properties.

Next in order of disposable wealth is the rapidly growing working class, which consists of about 4,000 families, probably half of which have migrated into the area from the poorer Castilian-speaking areas of Spain. Although this class owns none of the means of production, the high wages dictated by a labor shortage in Catalonia allow its members to live comfortably if modestly. This class has three major divisions: Skilled laborers, including office workers, who are generally Catalans, make up about half of the labor force; another 45 percent are the recently arrived Castilian migrants who man the new factories of the Alto Panadés; and a small (approximately 200 families) but significant minority works as agricultural laborers on estates that have phased out sharecropping. This is by far the most rapidly growing class in the district and reflects the increasing proletarianization of the Alto Panadés

Finally, another 4,000 families are basically sharecroppers *(rabassaires)*, who make the bulk of their living working the lands of the bourgeoisie for shares of the harvest. It is common for a sharecropper to own also a small plot of 1 or 2 hectares, in vineyard or garden or both. This class is suffering the most from the stagnancy of the wine trade and the modernization of agrarian estates now taking place in the Alto Panadés. Once the wheel horse of the viniculture industry, this class is now being gradually absorbed into the proletariat as machines replace men and as youth grows increasingly disenchanted with agriculture. All of the six villages in the district whose populations have declined in the last twenty years are dominated by sharecropping; another fifteen have had stationary populations during the same period, while the villages nearest to industrial developments have grown rapidly during the same period *(Ponencia de Población* (1966:4–5). This class, a remnant of the nineteenth-century prosperity of viniculture, is headed for extinction, as we shall see in Chapter 3.

Modernization is redefining the class structure of the Alto Panadés. It is eliminating the *rabassaires*, weakening sections of the petite bourgeoisie, vastly expanding the proletariat, and reorienting the economic activities of the haute bourgeoisie. Because the dynamics of class relationships have provided much of the political history of the Alto Panadés, this study must examine the emergent class structure and its not inconsiderable strains. Class tensions may be kept in check by the government, but they are evident in new forms, nonetheless, for all who are willing to observe them.

2

Growth of modern Catalonian regionalism

Of Spanish regional diversity, Ortega y Gasset (1937:41) wrote: "Spain is today not so much a nation as a series of water-tight compartments." He was despairing of the difficulties of national political integration that were created by the disparate nature of the regions making up the Spanish body politic. Radical differences in level of economic development, social structure, and cultural tradition have often set the regions in conflict with each other, just as they have fostered conflicts between the state and the regions. The terms "Spain" and "Spaniard" have much more reality for cartographers and demographers than for politicians and political analysts. For the latter, the terms have two diametrically opposed meanings: The first expresses an administrator's utopia of an orderly territory bulwarked by a loyal citizenry; the second encapsulates the realities of age-old conflicts and generations of rebels. Thus the contemporary political sociologists Juan Linz and Amando de Miguel (1966) define not one, but eight, Spains. In a similar vein, Prime Minister Cánovas, writing in exasperation at the end of the nineteenth century, defined Spaniards by default as "*los que no pueden ser otra cosa*" ("those who couldn't be anything else") (Brenan 1962:41).

Within Spain, no region has constituted for so long as grave a threat to the utopia of national unity as has Catalonia. Ortega's lament could have been written by the conde duque de Olivares[1] in the early seventeenth century, as he impotently watched the Catalans prepare a major revolt against the Hapsburg monarchy in which he held supreme power (Elliott 1963a). Then, the issue was whether the state could impose its hegemony over the Catalans or whether the Catalans would secede and attempt to reconstitute the independent nation they had created over five centuries previously (Trueta 1946; Elliott 1963a). Today, the issue is much the same: Catalans, regardless of social class, generally view themselves as a

24

people alienated from Spain and sorely oppressed by the central government. Unwilling subjects, not euphoric statists, are the people discussed in this work. It is remarkable enough that the political struggle between the Catalans and the state should have the same expression today that it had three centuries ago. Even more remarkable than the perpetual region-state conflict, however, is the institutional integrity of Catalan society that has survived in its major outlines for some nine centuries. For example, the major Catalan social institutions dealt with in this study – the *rabassa morta* contract, the *hereu-pubilla* marriage-inheritance system, and the emphasis on voluntarism – were already established in Catalonia by the late Middle Ages. That they have survived for so long is in itself noteworthy; that they have been able to survive, in addition to the chronic battle with the Spanish state, radical economic transformations, endemic class conflict, and natural catastrophes seems little short of miraculous. This institutional longevity impels scholars of contemporary Catalonia to probe history because contemporary Catalans act out, often quite self-consciously, what they take to be their historical impulses. Catalonia is a place where, to borrow from Karl Marx (1955:247), "the tradition of all the dead generations weighs like a nightmare on the brain of the living."

To point out that many key institutions of regional society originated in the Middle Ages is not to suggest that Catalonia is in any meaningful sense of the word "feudal." Indeed, scholarly opinion almost unanimously agrees that Catalan society has been precocious within the context of European history. Its precocity resides in the fact that at various junctures in its history, Catalonia has anticipated, even generated, the major outlines of the world transformation created by northern European industrial capitalism in the nineteenth and twentieth centuries. Thus, for Pierre Vilar (1962:I:421 and passim), perhaps the paramount historian of Catalan society, Catalonia of the eleventh and twelfth centuries constituted politically the prototype of the modern nation state (see also Trueta [1946]). And long before enclosure acts and satanic mills dominated England, as Eric Wolf (1959:158–9) points out, at the end of the fifteenth century, Catalonia stood on the brink of an industrial revolution based, as in England, on the manufacture of textiles. And the prime mover of these developments was the first true bourgeoisie. Catalonia was, in short, a prematurely bourgeoisified society, doomed to eclipse by the more powerful (and more feudal) Castilians.

Though Catalan social institutions are often treated in this context, their survival has less to do with their initial avant-garde character than with the continuity of certain broad structural political and economic conditions that transcend historical epochs, such as feudalism and capitalism. For example, Catalan economic productivity has for centuries been small-scale and dispersed, irrespective of what was cultivated in the countryside or manufactured in the towns and cities at any given moment. Key productive units were then (and were until recently) *families*, regardless of the type of productivity engaged in. Given the scale of production and its familial organization, it is not surprising that close attention should be paid to matters of marriage and inheritance in both the fourteenth and twentieth centuries. But this does not mean that the structural arrangements surrounding marriage and inheritance were put to precisely the same ends in these two different periods. We need not assume that a feudal lord of the fourteenth century married off his sons or daughters according to the *hereu-pubilla* system for the same reasons that a nineteenth-century bourgeois did. As will be argued throughout the text, Catalan institutions are adaptable because of both their complexity and their generalized nature.

Politically, Catalonia has not only been subject to a stormy relationship with the state (regardless of form), but has also suffered class warfare within. In the countryside, the issue of land tenure has long sparked unrest, leading the peasantry into civil war against the nobility in the fifteenth century, into chronic banditry and anarchy in the sixteenth to eighteenth centuries, into three Carlist wars against the bourgeoisie in the nineteenth century, and into a briefly successful social revolution against the same bourgeoisie in 1936 (Brenan 1962; Elliott 1963a; Giralt i Raventós 1964; Hansen 1969). In Barcelona, the frequent realities and perpetual threat of mob action turned by the late nineteenth century into working-class revolutionism paralleled in modern European history only in the Vryborg district of Saint Petersburg in 1917 (Trotsky 1937; Brenan 1962).

Against this backdrop of class warfare, it is nearly a miracle that anything that could be properly called a society developed in Catalonia. Even more unlikely is the development of a Catalan ruling class with historical continuity, organizational coherence, and genuine claims to regional hegemony. That such a society and such a ruling class undeniably developed is in large measure due to the viability of the regional social institutions that are the subject of this study. Much of the viability of these institutions resides in the fact that they provide a strong counterbalance to class conflict in both ideological and structural ways. Indeed, the strengths of these institutions lie in their eminently political nature. They are political in the Aristotelian sense of the term; that is, concerned with the ordering of relationships between groups in society. Viewed in this light, the *rabassa morta* contract becomes more than a simple juridical vehicle providing for the cultivation and harvesting of grapes; it is elevated to the realm of a social contract that stresses the partnership between landlord and peasant, a partnership deemed to benefit both. Similarly, the *hereu-pubilla* marriage-inheritance system is not only concerned with the regulation of family structure and the distribution of property, it is also a strategy of social mobility for all Catalans, rich and poor alike.

A cardinal feature of Catalan institutional life is an emphasis on voluntarism, of which formal contract is the supreme (though not the only) expression. Each party to a land-tenure agreement or to a marriage, every member of any public association, is there by personal choice. The obligations and rights of parties to contract are spelled out in infinite detail, lending formality and sobriety to the principle of free choice. Hence, in theory, the strength of Catalan society resides, not in hierarchical principles of dominance and subordination, but in cumulative cohesion wrought from an infinite series of individual acts of volition.

Rather than providing further evidence of the premature bourgeoisification of Catalonia, this ideological emphasis on voluntarism reflects some long-standing facts of power in the region. As mentioned above, Catalan society has been marked by sharp class divisions and conflicts. Because the regional upper class has not been able to guarantee the support of the Spanish state and because of the fragmented economic and political nature of the region, the popular classes have always had a greater measure of power in Catalonia than in other regions of Spain. Thus, merely to maintain itself, the Catalan ruling class has continuously had to work out its relationship with the regional popular classes in ways that would neutralize class conflict. Voluntarism is one means to this end because it allows the formation of alliances between sworn enemies. Generally lacking the means to coerce the popular classes to do its bidding, the Catalan ruling class has had to entice them to do so through the instruments of voluntarism.

Voluntarism, with its implications of both moral and economic rationalism, is counterposed against class interest, which is another form of economic rationalism. A logical culmination of these two equally strong ideological components operating in the same society might be a bitter division between Benthamite utilitarians and social revolutionaries. Catalonia has produced more than her share of both; yet Catalan society as a whole seems ambivalent toward these extremes and manages to exist in a state of permanent tension between the two. Indeed, it is not rare to encounter individuals who have vacillated between these poles in their recent political lives; many people are permanently torn between Catalan nationalism, which still is predicated on voluntarism (and, implicitly, on property), and one or another form of marxism. More than once in the course of fieldwork, the same individual expounded to me both positions at nearly the same time and with equally convincing sincerity. And every serious political party in the region in recent history has faced the impossible task of synthesizing these positions or at least trying to reconcile them.

A cardinal reason for this ambivalence is that behind the sober rationality of Catalan culture an enormous amount of symbolic overlay tends to derange this very rationality. This symbolic overlay is built into Catalonian institutions; like rationalism, this symbolic overlay is a feature of the ideology surrounding the purely instrumental aspects of these institutions. It imbues the daily routine, lived as it is within institutional constraints, with transcendental and mythic qualities. These qualities penetrate the emotional foundations of every Catalan: They orient love and family (through the *hereu-pubilla* system), work (through *rabassa morta*), and the web of interpersonal relations (through both of the above and the voluntary associations). The impact of these traits cannot be underestimated because Catalan society has long been predicated on personal lines; it simply is not a "mass society." What heightens the power of routine experience is that it is constantly under threat, from within and from without. This has led in turn to an efflorescence of Catalan folk culture, which is centered on a long series of collective events that glorify the homeland. Typical of these events are the *sardana* (a type of dancing), the erection of human towers, and pilgrimages to the Abbey of Montserrat. Anyone who has witnessed these activities can entertain no doubts that, at least at these moments, to be a Catalan is a religious experience.

Many of the themes touched upon so far appear in direct contradiction with each other. It is quite true that Catalan life is full of contradictions and, indeed, must be studied within a dialectical framework. Yet we are left with the unenviable task of making sense of these contradictions, of fitting them into a pattern. The pattern itself is not static; it is a coherent historical trajectory of a complex people. What follows is less an exposition of Catalan history than an outline of the emergence of this pattern.

The Middle Ages: prelude
to nineteenth-century industrial revolution

Modern Catalan history – the part that is concerned with the roots of the nineteenth-century industrial revolution and the creation of the Catalan bourgeoisie – has its origins in the struggle between Christendom and Islam for control of what is now southern France and the Iberian peninsula. In the annals of Castilian history, which searches for the elusive sources of Spanish nationhood, these nearly eight centuries (711–1492) of border struggles are iconoclastically referred to as the Reconquest. Common to both histories are the facts of failed nations and aborted empires, despite the promise of both political forms (Wallerstein, 1974b). Viewed from the pinnacles of power, the history of Catalonia or of Spain is one of heartbreak, of visionary but frustrated designs. A peasant, a worker, or a small businessman views this same history, with great accuracy, as one of uncontrolled change and uncertainty, fraught with dangers and possibilities. This amalgamation of fear and potential has often brought Spain to the forefront of Western history, as a place where issues are first posed, debated, and then somehow resolved in the wrong fashion. The Spanish Republic, culminating in fascism, is only a capstone to a long series of debates about political forms and goals.

Catalonia's experiment with early nation-statehood and empire began with the Reconquest, a process that took roughly two centuries (800–1000) to complete (Vilar 1962:I:370–95 and passim).

The grand design of this early nationhood evolved from an interplay of geography and timing. The expulsion of the Moors left a territory ranging from just north of Montpellier to just south of Valencia free from the Christian-Muslim struggles in the rest of Iberia as well as from the barbarian disturbances of northern Europe. Not only was this incipient maritime nation relatively free from political disturbances, but it was also in the hands of a people already unified by a common language and articulated by complex interdependent trading relationships (Vilar 1962:I:395).

A cursory examination of the topography of early Catalonia demonstrates a fairly neat correspondence between national boundaries and the Mediterranean littoral, suggesting that an ecological definition of the region is as appropriate as a political definition. The heartland of the region is the littoral, with its infinite mountain passes and valleys. The supreme expression of this heartland are the major port cities – Montpellier, Barcelona, Tarragona, Valencia – among which are strung out myriad minor ports (Trueta 1946). It is evident that Catalonia had to become an archetypical commercial nation, with its essential interests lying in the trans-Mediterranean trade. Though this orientation led to the development of not only a nation but a Catalan empire as well by the eleventh century, it proved a source of Catalan dissolution by the sixteenth century, when Castile's interest shifted to the Atlantic trade (Elliott 1963b:524).

However vital the trans-Mediterranean trade was for Catalonia, the region also served as an important trade conduit between Muslim Iberia and France at a time when north and central European economies were seriously disrupted by barbarian invasions (Bloch 1966:I:3 ff.). As Vilar (1962:I:395) suggests, the importance of this trade has been underestimated because of its diffuse nature. The principal items of trade were (1) a wide variety of agricultural products grown within Catalonia and (2) slaves obtained from coastal piracy. These items were funneled through the Pyrenean passes that bisect Catalonia, with Muslim gold serving as the initial medium of exchange. By the eleventh century, however, Catalonia became the first Iberian region to mint its own coinage to expedite this trade (Vilar 1962:I:395).

A third important stimulus to the commercial growth of medieval Catalonia was the development of the wool trade within the Iberian peninsula itself. This trade evolved as Castilian pastoralists wrested more and more border territories from the Moors. As the Reconquest of Castile progressed, more and more land became available for sheep raising, and, consequently more and more wool became available for Catalan textile producers and merchants. By 1278, with the organization of the *mesta*, the stockmen's guild that coordinated the trans-Iberian sheep runs, Catalan cities became the designated terminal points for these runs. Both the increasing volume of sheep and the political regularization of the pastoral cycle encouraged the growth of a textile industry that came to form the heart of Catalonia's trans-Mediterranean trade. By 1250, when Catalonia was at her territorial apogee, she had trading rights in Sicily, Africa, Asia Minor, Egypt, Flanders, and Champagne (Vilar 1962:I:408).

What distinguished Catalonia from coeval Mediterranean city-states was that the development of commerce was not limited to a single emerging metropolitan port. Although Barcelona underwent spectacular growth during this period, the evolution of the textile trade was reflected by a parallel growth of provincial Catalan cities. Far from remaining isolated agrarian backwaters of maritime Catalonia, provincial towns were incorporated into the mainstream of an economic structure that embraced the entire nation. For example, Vilafranca del Panadés, although it is an inland town 30 miles from the ports of Tarragona and Barcelona, had by the fifteenth century grown to be the eighth largest city in Catalonia, with a population of 4,000 (Giralt i Raventós 1966:15). Nor was the experience of Vilafranca unique: Early wool manufacture was both expressly rural and widespread, leading to the creation of the first great fortunes in the Catalan hinterland. The importance of these rural fortunes is amply illustrated by the fact that the Catalans who became such prominent advisors, magistrates, ambassadors, and administrators for the Aragonese crown in the thirteenth and fourteenth centuries were from the interior of Catalonia, rather than from Barcelona (Vilar 1962:I:425 ff.).

The growth of trade and the evolution of a merchant class were accompanied by concomitant political growth in Catalonia, expressed in the development of numerous institutions created to further commercial activity and/or to define the relationship of Catalonia with the kingdom of Aragon. Many of these institutions, such as the *Consolat de Mar*, which regulated maritime activities, or the *Consolat de Probi Homini*, the Barcelona merchants' association, or even Barcelona's municipal system have their analogs in most other Mediterranean city-states. Unique to Catalonia, however, was the long-standing pact between the emergent Catalan bourgeoisie and the Catalan feudal dynasty in Aragon. Since the beginning of the thirteenth century, each had supported the other's respective economic and political aims, while simultaneously maintaining its autonomy. This relationship became formalized with the creation of the Catalan Cortes, charged with legislating the terms of Catalan-Aragonese alliance, with particular emphasis on the fiscal arrangements between the two entities. It is worth noting that no other European power at that time had a political institution that included the legislative function, periodicity, and conditionality in its fiscal relationships with the crown (Vilar 1962:I:439).

That the defense of Catalan autonomy would be the primary concern of the Cortes was clear from the first meeting of the representatives of this body, held in Vilafranca del Panadés in 1218. The representatives met to vote on the royal subsidy, and voted upon it favorably only after the king agreed to satisfy Catalan plaints against the crown. The Catalan plaints of that meeting were to be issued for centuries in one form or another; they dealt with questions of monetary intervention (i.e., protection of Catalan coinage), demands for tariff protection in Catalan textile manufacture, rights to form corporate political institutions, and control over non-Christian populations in Catalonia (ultimately a matter of rights of taxation of these populations) (Vilar 1962:I:441). From this point forward, representatives of the crown of Aragon (and later of Castile) who sought to extend their authority into Catalonia or to increase taxation found themselves thwarted by parliamentary maneuvers, expressed in the series of constitutions generated by the Cortes, and bogged down hopelessly in interminable negotiations (Elliott 1963a). Political autonomy was further symbolized by the fact that the king of Aragon was not permitted to maintain permanent residence in Barcelona (Vilar 1962:I:429 ff., 439–42).

The conflict between the dynasty in Aragon and the Catalan merchants went much deeper than a struggle between political entities. At its root lay a conflict between vastly different economic orders: on the one hand, the growth of commerce and the merchant class, centered in the provincial cities and Barcelona; on the other, a seigneurial economy in the countryside, dominated by political and juridical feudalism, whose political expression was the crown. Thus the prototypical nation-state, which had generated political and commercial breakthroughs earlier than any other in Europe, also rested on a foundation of regressive feudalism. This early struggle between these two orders within Catalonia itself presaged a similar struggle between Catalonia and Castile several centuries later.

Yet Catalan feudalism was not classic European feudalism; nor did it resemble the feudalism that was evolving in other Iberian regions. In the first place, large estates never developed in Catalonia. Here again, regional ecology played a decisive role in the shaping of Catalan society. In contrast to the monotonous and barren landscapes of Castile and Aragon, two areas where the large estate was rapidly established, Catalonia is a land of small mountain valleys (with considerable topographical variation within the valleys) and with a poor subsoil that does not lend itself to the monoculture associated with the development of the estate (Vilar 1962:I:382–3). The varied terrain of these mountain valleys stimulated polyculture and consequently limited the size of property that could be effectively worked by family units. Catalonia quickly came to be a land characterized by distinctive *comarcas*, small areas of countryside with distinctive topographical features and modes of production peculiar to these areas. In turn, the development of polyculture both stimulated the growth of internal and external markets for a wide variety of agricultural products and underwrote much of the growth of Catalan cities and provincial towns (Vilar 1962:I:382).

We may speculate that the distinctive ecology of Catalonia, and the relative weakness of the feudal order and the crown in the first three centuries after the Reconquest, led to the development of the *hereu-pubilla* marriage-inheritance system, which rapidly became one of the social foundations of the Catalan nobility. Under this system, a single heir or heiress received de jure control of all immobile familial property at the time of his or her marriage and all other heirs received a share of movable properties and capital. Thus a large, mobile population of second sons and daughters with some available capital was created to enter into nonagricultural pursuits, which in turn spurred the development of Catalan commerce (Maspons i Anglasells 1931; Vilar 1962:I:395). This system was known in Catalonia prior to the year 1000, long before any form of primogeniture developed in northern Europe (Vilar 1962:I:394; Bloch 1966:I:204).

Although the development of the *hereu-pubilla* marriage-inheritance system both defined and strengthened the emergent Catalan nobility, the concomitant imposition of serfdom on the Catalan peasantry carried the seeds of destruction of this same nobility. Indeed, the nobles' attempt to enslave the peasantry and the peasantry's stout resistance to serfdom exemplify the endemic rural conflict that has characterized the Catalan countryside until the present. Juridically, the bones of contention in the feudal version of this conflict were the "six evil uses," the nobles' pretended claims to peasant land and labor. Three of the uses were legal devices through which the nobility could expropriate the property of a hitherto free peasantry;[2] the other three required the payment of idemnities by the peasantry to the nobility. Of the six uses, the *remença*, which required the peasant to ransom himself from serfdom, often at a price set arbitrarily by his lord, is historically the most important because it provoked the greatest bitterness on the part of the peasantry and the greatest concern on the part of the crown (Hinojosa 1918:367).

Taken together, the uses constituted noble claims to absolute domination of land and labor in rural Catalonia. These claims to absolute power quickly led the nobility into conflict, not only with the peasantry, but also with the king, who feared that social conflict would erupt within the realm and that consolidation of noble power would come at the expense of that of the king (Merriman 1936:I:477–80). Thus, while the uses did not become generalized in rural Catalonia until the latter part of the twelfth century, royal intervention in questions of land tenure was a marked feature of the reign of James I (1213–76). Under this monarch, intervention came in the form of specific exemptions from the uses granted the peasantries of particular locales, a policy continued by every succeeding monarch until the final abolition of the uses in 1486 (Merriman 1936:I:480; Vilar 1962:I:388–95; Elliott 1963a:69).

Owing to the fortuitous combination of royal exemptions and the growing prosperity of the rural Catalan economy, the nobility was able to maintain itself more or less intact until near the end of the fourteenth century, when a series of natural and economic catastrophes led to its ultimate demise. Ironically, great economic prosperity (the early fifteenth century was the apogee of both royal and

bourgeois luxury in Catalonia), went hand in hand with demographic catastrophe (Vilar 1962:I:460–1, 472–6). From 1350 to
1492, the history of the Catalan countryside is one of unmitigated
disaster; plague, famine, emigration, and messianic movements
occurred at roughly ten-year intervals and led to the depopulation
of rural Catalonia.

Paced by the growing lack of manpower and the consequent
dwindling of seigneurial dues and rural productivity, the Catalan
nobility began to press harder for the implementation of the uses in
the face of royal and peasant opposition to these claims. As an
immediate result, the countryside by 1380 was engulfed in a series
of small-scale conflicts between landlords and tenants leading to a
full-scale civil war by 1462 (Hinojosa 1918:233–44; Merriman
1936:479–80; Elliott 1963a:4–5; Elliott 1963b:26–9). By 1448, Al-
fonso the Magnanimous was attempting to negotiate peace with the
peasants themselves; in 1455 he was forced temporarily to suspend
the uses altogether. During this period, the countryside had been
converted into a land of abandoned estates coveted equally by
peasant and lord. Indeed, by this time it seems academic to discuss
land-tenure arrangements and social classes in rural Catalonia, as
society had broken down into anarchic bandit chiefdoms.

Peasant unrest coupled with the opposition of the crown brought
about the downfall of the Catalan nobility. This downfall was also
aided by the merchant class, specifically by that segment engaged
in the wheat trade. Throughout the Middle Ages, the Catalan nobility's fortunes were closely tied to the price structure of both local
and regional wheat markets. Wheat for the market was grown in
virtually all *comarcas*, and each *comarca* vied with every other for
competitive market advantages.[3]

Although the nobility controlled the production of wheat, the
merchants purchased it and subsequently resold it in the marketplace. By the onset of the fifteenth century, wheat was already
overabundant on the market because of population decline. The
market was even further depressed by the merchants' habit of
importing Sicilian wheat, so that Catalan ships dispatched with
manufactures to that island would not return home empty (Giralt i
Raventós 1958). This and the subsequent regional economic contraction dealt a mortal economic blow to a nobility already confronted with shrinking seigneurial revenues and a rebellious
peasantry.

Finally, in 1486 after nearly a century and a half of rural conflict, the Catholic kings abolished the feudal order in Catalonia by the Decree of Guadalupe. This decree stipulated the devolution of administrative control of arable land to the serfs who tilled it. The serfs did not become outright owners of the land, however; they were required to pay their former lords an annual rent (Giralt i Raventós 1964:52–3). Thus, the nobles were converted into rentiers, and the serfs were turned into an essentially free peasantry. Or, as Giralt i Raventós (1964:52) puts it: "In this fashion [i.e., by virtue of the Decree of Guadalupe], by a simple twist of Civil Law, a redistribution of property occurred."

The socioeconomic impacts of the Decree of Guadalupe were, of course, far more complex than the decree itself intended. In the first place, many of the lesser lords had become so weakened by the periods of plague and low wheat prices that they were forced to sell their land outright to their former tenants. For example, in the Alto Panadés, various contemporary large estates on choice lands are held by the descendants of serfs who purchased the land directly from nobles between 1496 and 1552. The holdings thus purchased were often so large that the new landholders had to hire men to work them, thus creating the first rural proletariat in Catalonia (Giralt i Raventós 1958:163). Large landholders, including the church, sought to maintain themselves in the face of labor shortage by forming "establishments" with heritable rights to cultivation. These establishments ceded on choice portions of their domains in exchange for the payment of the annual rent and, in their provision for secure long-term tenure, anticipated the *rabassa morta* contract prevalent in the nineteenth and twentieth centuries. Looked at from a political perspective, the landlord-serf conflicts of the fourteenth and fifteenth centuries contributed two major features of contemporary Catalan land-tenure arrangements: (1) actual control of agriculture in the hands of tillers of the soil and (2) long-term land-tenure agreements between landlord and tenant.

Another major effect of the decree was to stimulate the commercial development of Catalan agriculture, for the decree broke down feudal barriers to the free flow of agricultural produce and to the sale of land itself. Land entered the market not as a simple commodity, like modern real estate, but as productive units that could be worked by one family or several in collaboration. In contrast to the hereditary basis of landownership in the feudal order, which simply passed on a tract of land through the generations regardless of its productive capacity, land was now transferred as vineyard, garden, forest, or wheatland, that is, according to what it produced. Similarly, the collection of both taxes and rent became marketable as well, creating new opportunities for the accumulation of capital in the countryside. We may speculate that at this point the *hereu-pubilla* marriage-inheritance system became generalized among all rural property-holding classes, not only as a means of retaining properties acquired, but as a conscious familial strategy for the accumulation of capital (see Chapter 4 for an extended discussion).

By the end of the feudal period and coeval with the discovery of the New World, Catalonia was already en route to becoming the commercial manufacturing region it is presently. Yet, just as the seeds of the institutional arrangements that fueled this growth had been sown, this prematurely modern society had already incorporated the lethal contradictions that were to plague it in the nineteenth and twentieth centuries.

Catalan decline:
the sixteenth and seventeenth centuries

At the dawn of the discovery and colonization of the New World, with its immeasurable resources and potentials, it would be logical to suppose that Spain, and Catalonia, had achieved political and economic greatness commensurate with the literary brilliance of the same period, the Golden Century.[4] American riches, particularly silver and gold, shored up depleted royal treasuries and stimulated Catalan manufacture and commerce. Catalonia, with internal peace ostensibly guaranteed by the Decree of Guadalupe, might recoup its population and productivity and benefit from new sources for trade in the Americas and from the help of a fortified royal navy in clearing the Mediterranean of the pirates who had disrupted overseas trade for more than a century (Elliott 1963a,b).

Yet the sixteenth and seventeenth centuries were a time of bitter illusion for both the Hapsburg Empire and the Catalans, leading to the bankruptcy of both and loss of territory by the latter. In retrospect, it is remarkable that in this period so many fantasies of power and grandeur were held to in the face of so much disorder and poverty. What endows much of the literature of the Golden Century with its poignancy is the treatment of this contradiction. In the picaresque genre exemplified by *Lazarillo de Tormes*, we witness the spectacle of a noble offering to his servant and himself a plate of air, served on elegant silver, consumed with all the elegance of *grandes señores*. And it is no accident that by 1605 Don Quixote, the disconnected knight symbolic of the state of affairs in Spain, had made his appearance, tilting in what he imagined to be the best chivalric tradition at windmills. It is especially noteworthy that for him Barcelona, with its long-standing tradition of commerce and its greedy bourgeoisie, had somehow become the embodiment of gentlemanly virtue and decorum (Vilar 1956). Thus a contemporary of Cervantes, Gonzalez de Cellorigo, could write of Spain at this time that "it truly seems that they tried to make this republic a republic of enchanted men who live outside the natural order of things" (Vilar 1956:11).

Central to the decline of the Iberian peninsula was the acquisition of the American Empire, which, coupled with the Holy Roman Empire, proved far too heavy an administrative and financial burden for Spain, let alone Castile, to bear (Wallerstein 1974a,b). The complexities of this enormous burden are well discussed elsewhere (Vilar 1962:I:863–5 and passim; Elliott 1963a,b; Wallerstein 1974a,b); they are briefly outlined here. For Castile, the Spanish seat of the Hapsburg monarchy, one immediate result was near depopulation, as countless people migrated to the New World in search of riches and others were dispatched as royal officials to the far corners of this world empire. Castile quickly became an area with no productive base whatever, in which the nobility attempted to live off rents and the remaining peasantry was increasingly ground down by continuously increasing taxes (Vilar 1962:I:565 ff.; Elliott 1963b:137–49). The monarchy was in even more precarious straits than Castile; by the 1500s, Charles V was embroiled in conflict in the Low Countries and with France. To underwrite the costs of administering the empire while simultaneously fighting long wars, the crown relied heavily on the flow of silver from the Americas and on numerous loans from the German banking house of the Fuggers. Throughout the reign of Charles V, the monarchy hovered each year on the brink of bankruptcy, which finally engulfed it in 1557 (Wallerstein 1974a:183).

For Catalonia, the results of empire were possibly even more disastrous than for Castile. In the first place, the crown's nearly absolute reliance on American silver and its concomitant emphasis on the trans-Atlantic trade led it to ignore the Mediterranean trade on which the commercial prosperity of Catalonia depended. Not only did the crown turn a deaf ear to the Catalan merchants' repeated requests for the royal navy to clear the Mediterranean of pirates, but it also excluded the Catalans from the trans-Atlantic trade, which became a monopoly of Seville (Elliott 1963a:544–5). Furthermore, the influx of American silver, coupled with the crown's repeated borrowing, had the effect of inflating the Catalan currency by means of periodic devaluations (Elliott 1963a:261–2). Far from rescuing Catalonia from the economic slump of the fourteenth century, crown policies of the sixteenth and seventeenth centuries plunged the region further into economic decline, from which it did not recover until the nineteenth century.

In the second place, the crown sought to augment its revenues by increasing taxes and other royal subsidies in Catalonia. Royal preoccupation with obtaining revenues from the Catalans reached its zenith in the reign of Philip IV (1621–65), whose favorite, Olivares, hatched all manner of schemes to induce or force the Catalans to fill the royal coffers (Elliott 1963b). Unfortunately for Olivares and the crown, such levies could not be collected without infringing upon the prerogatives of the Catalan government in Barcelona, prerogatives that were zealously guarded. From 1622 to 1640, relations between the crown and the Catalan government steadily deteriorated until the principality revolted in 1640 and placed itself under the protection of France, which was then at war with Castile.

The rebellion of the Catalans ultimately proved a disaster for the principality, which became a political pawn of the French in their long-standing conflict with the Hapsburgs. In 1659, when Spain and France negotiated a temporary end to twenty-four years of warfare, one of the terms of the Peace of Pyrenees was that Catalonia would be effectively cut in two, with the provinces of Cerdagne and Roussillon ceded to the French (Brenan 1962:26), thus forming the borders of modern Catalonia. The Catalans lost a large part of their homeland, although they managed to maintain regional autonomy until 1716, when the principality was forcibly incorporated into the Bourbon dynasty.

Catalonia resurgent:
the eighteenth and nineteenth centuries

Eighteenth century

Despite loss of both territory and political autonomy, Catalonia participated in the economic dynamism of the eighteenth century. What makes this new growth so extraordinary is that further war between France and Spain had completely disrupted the region's economy. The renaissance that took place was the result of what Vilar (1962:II:212) calls *fourmillement,* a remarkably dispersed, small-scale, antlike activity that led to a complete recuperation from the disasters of the fourteenth and fifteenth centuries by the 1730s. This period also saw the fruition of the commercial potential of the Decree of Guadalupe and the further generalization of the *hereu-pubilla* structure.

Powering the growth of eighteenth-century Catalonia was a surging agricultural economy created by a conjunction of high wine prices, abundant wheat harvest, and low food prices (Vilar 1962:II:555 ff.). During this period, the spread of vineyards foretold the nineteenth-century viticultural revolution. Vineyard was not new to Catalonia: Grapes had always been grown in small quantities in many rural *comarcas* for local consumption. However, grapes had always proved less remunerative than wheat, even during the fifteenth to seventeenth centuries, when the price of wheat was depressed. Catalan agriculturalists were supremely indifferent to vineyard as a source of revenue until the late seventeenth century. Illustrative of this indifference is a seventeenth-century anecdote from the Alto Panadés, later to become a quintessential viticulture region. In the account of Giralt i Raventós (1966:20–1), gleaned from local archives of the era, two gentlemen from Reus (province of Tarragona) solicited permission from the Vilafranca city hall to establish a brandy distillery in the town. Rather than exact the normal tributes for permission of this kind, the mayor merely requested that the gentlemen from Reus provide him with two capons and a glass of their brandy each Christmas day.

This lackadaisical attitude toward the fruits of the vine (monetary and otherwise) stands in sharp contrast to the tremendous expansion of viticultural lands in both the eighteenth and nineteenth centuries. In the eighteenth century, high prices were brought about by local scarcity, caused by the destruction of many vineyards during the wars and by exportation to northern Europe in exchange for salt fish and, later, textiles (Vilar 1962:II:557). According to Vilar (1962:II:378): "One understands that since each farmer planted grapes, that each bushy plot had been brought into cultivation by *rabassa morta* establishments and that cereals retreated before the vine that was often planted on land that was previously sown with wheat." Grape monoculture replaced traditional polyculture in Ampurdan, Tarragona, and even in some areas of the Panadés, including Vilafranca, where brandy continued to be distilled.

The *rabassa morta* contract, which had existed since the great regional prosperity of the Middle Ages, was revived at the end of the seventeenth century and with particular vigor in the eighteenth century. According to Vilar (1962:II:220): "It again became one of the fundamental agrarian institutions of the Catalan region. . . . In the second half of the century . . . the *rabassa morta* contract is defined . . . by a document of the *Patrimonio Real* as the 'sale of the right to plant grapes.' " Toward the end of the century the underlying ambiguity between commercialization and security of tenure appeared between landowners and *rabassaires*, setting the stage for the sharper class conflict of the late nineteenth century.

Grapes epitomize eighteenth-century growth and prosperity, but expansion extended to other agricultural products, including wheat, olives, and fruit trees. New *masia* lands were brought into cultivation; marshes and swamps were drained; dry lands were irrigated. Following this prosperity, the population doubled in less than sixty years, and new leases, including *rabassa morta*, were established. Though some agricultural initiative came from rural merchants and public notaries, most of it resulted from peasant efforts (Vilar 1962:II:42 ff. 212–56). This contrasts strongly with the agricultural growth of the nineteenth century, when the prime mover was the urban bourgeoisie with new and scientific commercial orientations. In fact, at the end of the eighteenth century, a notable from Moiá attributed most of the agricultural growth to the peasant, who

knows how to turn rocks into earth and to transport this from where there is an excess of earth, to where there is a lack of earth. The art of turning rocks into earth is practiced thus: first one must dig up the rocks from the fields, which are sterile because of them. If these rocks are red, or reddish, they must be pulled out with much labor and exposed to sun and frost for a few years, taking care to crush them and to turn them over periodically. They then transform themselves into fertile ground, and after several years, and after having been smoked, this earth is of as good a quality as any other [Vilar 1962:II:303]

Vilar (1962:II:303) comments that "this universal effort is quite striking."

It is important to recognize that especially at the beginning of the eighteenth century, all the new establishments were seigneurial. That is, tenure was based on seigneurial rents, and the increase in these rents formed the capital for subsequent commercial and industrial expansion. For the remaining great lords, this meant that their revenues quintupled. They had no expenses of production and probably reinvested very little in the region. But these lords did have collection expenses, and this revenue was spread among a multiplicity of tax-farming associations. One-quarter of these was managed by rich peasants, laborers, or laborer-merchants; another quarter was managed by businessmen or merchants, and the remaining half by rural or urban artisans. Tax farming provided a source of income to all these individuals; it was not a "capitalist accumulation, but provided Adam Smith's 'previous accumulation' from which real capitalism would ensue" in the late eighteenth and in the nineteenth centuries (Vilar 1962:II:574).

For the rich peasants or the *masia* holders the advantages offered by the eighteenth century were tremendous. First, their lands were the best, having been chosen during the period of depopulation after the Decree of Guadalupe in the fifteenth century. Second, the increase in rents in the early part of the century arose from the *multiplicity* of rents rather than more expensive rents. Thus these peasants were not overtaxed and had sufficient capital to invest in cattle and other improvements. The polyculture of eastern Catalonia was especially favored. Because of the variety of crops, the area never suffered any of the price declines or shortages of the monocultural vineyards. And the size of their holdings allowed the peasants to subdivide into additional establishments, at first of the traditional heritable type, but toward the end of the century into shorter and more commercial leases. Their income increased both on a rentier basis and on the basis of greater yield (Vilar 1962:II:57 ff.).

Also in contrast to the nineteenth century, the impetus to urban commerce or to the unification of the regional economy in the 1700s came from the rural regions. The mechanism for this connection was the *hereu-pubilla* inheritance system, which we have speculated became generalized among securely tenured peasants after the Decree of Guadalupe. The commercial potential of this system had been unfulfilled during the two preceding centuries of economic stagnation. But in the eighteenth century, owing to the combined impetus of high vinicultural prices, the multiplicity of tax-farming positions available, and increased commercial opportunities, younger sons were sent with some capital to establish themselves as professionals in the towns. Vilar has found myriad examples of joint business ventures between peasant householders and their younger sons, who were urban doctors, lawyers, and merchants. These modest urban professionals eventually formed the great cotton textile and commercial dynasties of Barcelona. "On the other hand," Vilar (1962:II:502) adds, "it is rare that the first generation reached the solid situation of 'matriculated businessmen' (i.e., in the *Junta de Commercio*). Occasionally the matriculated businessman is the son of a merchant, manufacturer, or artisan, and his agricultural wealth is of a recent origin."

The familial locus of Catalan commercial regeneration displayed the same antlike and dispersed quality as the agricultural rebirth of the eighteenth century. The basic structures of Catalan commerce were three: the *boutique*, or small shop; the *barca*, or joint association for shipbuilding and outfitting; and the *company*, or joint stock association. Each exhibited a tremendous dispersal of capital; the *boutique*, in particular, displayed a great potential for mobility and diversification, since it sold at retail to the public and at wholesale to other *boutiques*. A single enterpreneur could occasionally participate in all three. For instance, in 1717, Miguel Alegre started a *boutique* in Barcelona selling spices and imported textiles. As soon as Alegre (or any other *boutique* holder) had enough capital, he entrusted the store to an "administrator," often an employee or a relative, with whom he signed a *company* contract.[5] The *boutique* was now one of many enterprises in the original owner's *company*. Miguel Alegre's *company* was involved in the following businesses from 1717 to 1736: tax farming; provisioning of meat and wheat for the Barcelonian municipality; imports and exports of agricultural products, including the exchange of brandy for salt fish in northern Europe; shipbuilding *(barcas);*[6] and insurance. By 1736, the House of Alegre had become a great commercial enterprise, with an agent in Cádiz for colonial trade, a *boutique* in Madrid to tap the internal market, and agents in Amsterdam to buy textiles in exchange for brandies, thus supplementing the fish and brandy trade with England (Vilar 1962:III:384–412). While not all *boutique* holders attained the international success of the House of Alegre, many did. The system of shares, or joint stockholding, allowed the participation and advancement of the great and humble, in contrast to the more constricted bourgeois of the nineteenth century. Upward mobility was a fact of life for the eighteenth-century entrepreneur and became an article of ideological faith for the nineteenth-century bourgeois.

By midcentury, however, Catalonia had reached the limits of spontaneous agricultural and commercial growth. Yet the agricultural surge was maintained both by importing wheat to keep prices relatively low and by increasing exports of wine, this time to the American colonies, to keep wine prices high.[7] Another threat to the economy, relative overpopulation (by the 1750s), was absorbed twenty years later by the growing textile industry. By the 1770s Catalonia had again become the economic center of Spain, as exports and colonial trade combined to produce sustained economic growth (Vilar 1962:II:555–59; Vicens Vives 1969:600–1).

Catalonia's commercial situation was not entirely favorable at the end of the eighteenth century, however. Intensive regular trade between Catalonia and the colonies diminished the rate of profits; even profits from Mexican silver were quickly reduced by both rising salaries and meat purchases from over the Pyrenees. Additionally, the spread of North American and English exports to the Spanish colonies was lowering the prices for Catalan manufactured goods there. More and cheaper industrial products were needed (Vilar 1962:III:559–66).

A solution to this dilemma was provided by a resurgent textile industry, dormant since the Middle Ages. In the early eighteenth century the textile industry, which consisted mainly of the printing of calicoes, was but one of many possible enterprises for the joint stock associations. As one of their enterprises, these associations imported textiles. By midcentury, textile production and commerce diverged, and with the reaffirmed tariff protection accorded by the Spanish state, the Barcelonian elite became divided into two dominant and cooperating groups, the merchants and the calico manufacturers (Vicens Vives 1969:536–7). The calico manufacturers provide the prototype of the great Catalan bourgeoisie of the nineteenth century, the typical textile tycoons. But no one around them recognized in them the seeds of the industrial revolution. Thus Vicens Vives (1969:498) writes that "the appearance on the economic scene of manufacturers of calicos produced some priceless statements by the bureaucrats charged with classifying their activities. Since they did not fit into any of the established guides, the census put them down as 'idlers,' that is, unclassifiable. These 'idlers' were in fact the country's future." By 1772 their industrial distinctiveness was formalized by the foundation of the Cottonyarn Company, and by 1804 they attempted to break out of the cottage industry stage with a massive importation of machinery (Vicens Vives 1969:526). But, as had happened a century earlier, a decade of war and the loss of colonies halted further Catalan development until the early 1830s.

Nineteenth century

It is important to realize that the context of Catalan development was radically different in the nineteenth century from what it had been in the eighteenth. Spain, having lost most of its colonies, had become virtually a colony to other European powers. Andalusia exported wines and wheat to England in exchange for cheap manufactured goods; the Biscayan region became the domain of German, English, Belgian, and French steel industries (Vicens Vives 1969:658,662). Under these conditions, the Spanish state gave only sporadic tariff protection to Catalan textiles. With the loss of the American colonies, Spain became Catalonia's prime market; and Spain, with the option of cheaper foreign goods, increasingly attacked Catalan businessmen as "monopolists."[8] In the early part of the nineteenth century, during a period of protectionism, the Catalan bourgeoisie saw industry as the way to create the Spanish nation. Catalan books were published with titles such as *España con industria, rica y fuerte (Spain with Industry, Rich and Strong)*, and deputies exclaimed in the constitutional Cortes that the "poverty" of Catalonia would ruin Spain" (Vilar 1962:I:150). Later, however, their focus became entirely regional. By midcentury industrial interests and the interests of the raw materials exporters had diverged to the point that the Madrid Chamber of Commerce was financing vicious press campaigns against Catalonia. A speaker at the Madrid League of Free Exchange spoke of the Catalan businessmen as "birds of prey . . . of unbridled voracity . . . famished wolves which devour the substance of all Spaniards . . . monopolists . . . bedouins . . . gallows birds whose heads we would like to see pilloried in a public place" (Vilar 1962:I:151–2). Though the economics of Catalonia and Spain in the nineteenth century were extremely complex, this tension between the Spanish dependency elites and the Catalan bourgeoisie must be regarded as the basic context in which to understand the peculiarities of the nineteenth-century Catalan development.

The spectacular growth of industry in Catalonia during the nineteenth century has been described many times, with particular emphasis on the growth of Barcelona (e.g., Vicens Vives 1961; Brenan 1962:28–30). The impact of this industrial revolution on the Catalan countryside is less well understood. Much attention has been paid to the role of the merchant entrepreneur in the rise of Catalan industry; less attention has been paid to the relationship of the rural entrepreneur to his urban counterpart. Much of the coherence of modern Catalan regionalism was provided by a social merger and concentration of rural and urban entrepreneurs during the economic colonization of the countryside by the latter.

In large measure the colonization of the countryside was a direct function of certain weaknesses of the Catalan industrial economy. Although the progress of Catalan industry during the century was spectacular, it was not linear, but subject to fits and starts. Lack of credits and steady markets in the interior of Spain,[9] in addition to the disruptions of wars and internal political upheavals, made industrial growth and prosperity in Catalonia cyclical phenomena (Vicens Vives 1961:127–9). The pronounced economic cycles created periodic havoc among Catalan industrialists, whose small textile factories were frequently ruined by slumps.

Faced with the vagaries of the industrial economy and the lack of political support from Madrid, Catalan entrepreneurs had to diversify their economic holdings to safeguard against bankruptcy caused by the downward cycles of the industrial economy. In their efforts to find stable sources of wealth, most Catalan entrepreneurs turned toward the acquisition of various types of rental properties, especially after 1850. None of the rental schemes proved so profitable as investments in rural properties (Vicens Vives 1961:57–8). Speculation in land had been common at the end of the eighteenth century. After the Napoleonic wars and a period of recuperation, agricultural prices continued to rise.

In part, the rise in price of agrarian produce was a function of the rapid growth of the city of Barcelona,[10] whose burgeoning need for food alone might have been sufficient to maintain the rural economy. Wheat, corn, potatoes, rice, barley, and olives all became widely produced in rural Catalonia, as rural expansion continued. Various crops were produced in such abundance that they were also exported to other European countries: By 1890 potatoes from the district of Mataró were well known all over the Continent (Vicens Vives 1961:68).

As profitable as these crops were, they were much less remunerative than grapes, which by the end of the nineteenth century were to be found in every Catalan *comarca* save those of the high Pyrenees (Vicens Vives 1961:54). Vineyard continued to be highly profitable. Its expansion, begun in the eighteenth century, continued either spreading at the expense of other crops or extending into lands that had hitherto lain uncultivated. According to Vicens Vives (1961:65), "The expansion of vineyard knew no limits, occupying not only the forests, bluffs and hillsides, but also cultivated fields, until then dedicated to grains . . . the clear fact is, that between 1850 and 1865, and in spite of the invasion of oidium [a fungal disease of grapes], the expansion of vineyard in the Panadés surpassed the maximum of the three previous centuries."

Despite the loss of most of the American colonies, Catalonia continued to export wines to Cuba and the Philippines, and domestic consumption continued to expand. The profits from the wine trade were so great at the end of the nineteenth century that they were nearly as important as textiles in accounting for the prosperity of Catalonia.

The agricultural growth of the first half of the nineteenth century contrasts with that which followed 1850. Up to that time, growth was a continuation of the eighteenth-century pattern of small-scale expansion. After 1850 the impetus came from the urban bourgeoisie, with an assortment of new and more advanced agricultural techniques. Behind this expansion into agriculture was the 1849 abolition of protection for Spanish industry. Even though the Catalan textile industry continued more or less protected,[11] textile production slumped in 1850 (Vicens Vives 1961:91). Simultaneously various disentailment laws put large quantities of church lands on the market at low prices, providing an opportunity for nervous industrialists, anxious to protect their positions, to acquire land.

The recolonization of the countryside was carried out initially by three discrete social groupings, which later merged into one. Vicens Vives is unclear regarding the respective roles of urban rural investors. He states (1961:60) that these investors were (1) moneyed aristocrats, (2) the metropolitan bourgeoisie, and (3) wealthy nonaristocratic landholders. Yet elsewhere (1961:58), he attributes the principal role in the colonization to "rural gentry, who with one foot in the countryside and the other in the city, breathed the renovating air of the science of their times."

This contradiction is only apparent, however, because eighteenth-century Catalan agriculture and commerce tended to unify merchants and rural landholders. Although various social groups engaged in land speculation, the economics of colonization following 1850 welded them into a single coherent force, held together by ties of kinship and economic interest. A concentration of the urban and industrial bourgeoisie is apparent in the genealogies of the 1840s (Vicens Vives 1961:196), and by the end of the century, twenty or thirty families formed the political and economic leadership of the region. These were, according to Vicens Vives (1961:194–5), "the men who said yes or no," the men who ran Catalonia. The nature of the rural recolonization produced a wealthy bourgeoisie whose members had (and still have) both rural and urban investments. As a social counterpart of their diversified investments, the same family came to have branches living in both the city and the countryside.

Various pieces of evidence suggest how this merger and colonization took place. First, from about the middle of the nineteenth century, titles of nobility were accorded both urban and rural wealthy entrepreneurs, allowing them access to the salons of the Spanish nobility (Vicens Vives 1961:166).[12] Second, the merger between these groups was evident in the foundation of the Agrarian Institute of San Isidro in 1859. Both aristocrats and metropolitan bourgeoisie were well represented in this group, which was largely responsible for the diffusion of new agrarian techniques throughout the countryside. It is a curious fact that none of these new techniques developed in the nineteenth century was developed in the countryside: All mentioned by Vicens Vives (1961:59–61) were developed in Barcelona and attest to the agrarian interests of the Catalan manufacturers of that era. Barcelona manufacturers of nitrogen fertilizers, iron plows, and chemicals for treating crops belonged to the Agrarian Institute of San Isidro, which relayed these items to the rural *comarcas*.

Third, and perhaps most important, was the continuing operation of the *hereu-pubilla* system of inheritance. Apart from the juridical underpinnings of this marriage-inheritance system were other implicit social features. The essence of this system was that the firstborn child was to maintain the wealth accumulated by his parents; all succeeding offspring were to increase it (Maspons i Anglasells 1935:51). The role of the principal heir was obvious; the other male offspring were supposed to use their inheritance money to establish businesses in their own rights. Various Catalan writers have suggested that this institution actually created many of the dynamic entrepreneurs of the nineteenth as well as the eighteenth centuries (Maspons i Anglasells 1935; Vicens Vives 1961). Particular attention has been focused on the entrepreneurial activities of the second sons of rural landholders; frequently these second sons became small industrialists in Barcelona (Maspons i Anglasells 1935:59). In short, not only did the metropolitan bourgeoisie shore up its fortunes by investing in agrarian properties, but the rural gentry used the marriage-inheritance system to acquire industrial properties in the cities.

In spite of the apparent potential for economic independence enjoyed by each businessman or large landholder, and for the formation of a multiplicity of small to medium-sized businesses, there can be little doubt that in the nineteenth century the *hereu-pubilla* system functioned both to concentrate wealth and to consolidate the bourgeoisie socially. It merged all familial holdings. The branches of a given family, irrespective of where they were located, were always in contact with one another and acted as a single unit (Vicens Vives 1961:185–6). All shared their knowledge of commerce and their personal contacts, backed each other financially, and shared in the proceeds of the familial ventures. Through the unity of the family created by the *hereu-pubilla* system, the bourgeoisie was able to unify itself and to have one foot in the countryside and the other in the cities (Vicens Vives 1961:192–3).

But however socially and economically coherent the Catalan bourgeoisie became during the transformation of the countryside, class unity was not the sole reason for its success. The colonization of the countryside brought these people into conflict with the established rural interests in the form of the church and segments of the peasantry (Brenan 1962:28). Though the Decree of Guadalupe destroyed the Catalan feudal nobility, it did not dispossess the church of its considerable rural properties. Church lands were worked by peasants under long-term contracts (Vicens Vives 1961:52). And both church and peasants resented the speculation in lands by the bourgeoisie and saw in it a threat to their own economic security. In the years following 1828, a cycle of industrial and commercial prosperity included speculation in rural properties. The church and the peasantry under its control began to mobilize for a struggle against the bourgeoisie. In 1833 the First Carlist War broke out, taking the form of skirmishes between the national army and the peasantry.[13] During this war (1833–40) and the Second Carlist War (1845–49), the national government passed the disentailment acts mentioned earlier, divesting the church of its holdings.[14] These acts intensified the pace of land speculation and, therefore, the colonization of the countryside by the expanding bourgeoisie (Vicens Vives 1961:59).

Although these acts speeded the colonization, the bourgeoisie still faced a hostile countryside in which the Carlists sporadically offered armed resistance until 1876.[15] The emerging bourgeoisie was able to press its claims by force: Both the national militia and the *guardia civil* (a rural political police force) were instrumental in the pacification of Carlist elements. Even if the militia and the *guardia civil* could have annihilated the Carlists, the problems of colonization would not have been solved, for the bourgeoisie was dependent upon the Carlist peasantry as a labor force to work its newly acquired fields.

The principal problem for the Catalan bourgeoisie, after Carlism had been defeated as a political force in the countryside, was to recruit Carlist peasants to tend the vineyards under conditions that would promote the peasants' loyalty to their landlords. The instrument used by the bourgeoisie was the *rabassa morta* sharecropping system. The nineteenth-century *rabassa morta* contract was a long-term rental agreement between landholder and sharecropper, which charged the sharecropper with planting and maintaining vineyards for the life of the vines (about fifty years). In return for the use of the landholder's property, the sharecropper paid the landlord one-third of the harvest (Hansen 1969:214). In short, the contract was designed to fix the cultivator on the soil for a long period, thus avoiding the economic insecurities of short-term contracts.[16]

As the juridical instrument of the colonization of the countryside, the *rabassa morta* proved successful. Attracted by the long-term tenure guaranteed by the contract and by the high profit from viticulture, colonists flocked into vineyard districts. Initially, the contract was fairly effective in assuring the loyalty of the sharecroppers to their landlords, both economically and politically. After the last Carlist war, the countryside was quiet; the *rabassaires* began to absorb some of the regionalist ideology then expressed by their landlords and were receptive to the bourgeois *caciques* (bosses). However, toward the end of the nineteenth century, a deterioration of economic conditions in the countryside led to the growth of a bitter class struggle between *rabassaires* and proprietors (Vicens Vives 1961:66) (see Chapter 3 for discussion of this conflict).

Thus, within the context of Spanish hostility to Catalan industry, the Catalan bourgeoisie diversified its holdings, returning to wine to protect itself against the fluctuations of the industrial economy. The destruction of French viticulture by phylloxera (a type of plant louse) gave bourgeois and peasant alike fifteen years of dizzying agricultural profits. But the decade of the 1890s that saw both the destruction of Catalan vines by phylloxera and the loss of the Cuban and Philippine agricultural and industrial markets exposed the contradictions implicit in the system of regional land tenure.

Some political dimensions of modern Catalonia

The Catalan industrial revolution and agrarian transformation brought in their train two main tendencies that marked the political history of the region from the 1850s until the end of the Spanish civil war. The first was the dramatic reorganization of Catalan society, which sparked a wave of regionalist sentiment manifested in the growth of voluntary associations. These voluntary associations were varied in nature, but all served to glorify regional culture. These glorifications of regional culture, taken collectively, offered the potential of welding all peoples of the Catalan cultural tradition into one movement, irrespective of their social conditions. The political thrust of this movement was directed toward gaining political autonomy for the region, either in the form of home rule or by secession from Madrid.

The second major political tendency in Catalonia was a bitter struggle among social classes that the cyclic nature of the economy tended to exacerbate. This tendency was marked by the growth of revolutionary political parties and syndicalism in Barcelona, and was characterized by assassinations, strikes, and ever-increasing militancy on the part of the metropolitan proletariat. Class conflict was not confined to Barcelona. It also appeared in the growing conflict between *rabassaires* and landholders in the countryside that began in 1890. Both sets of class conflicts intensified throughout the twentieth century until they crystallized in the revolution of July 1936 (Brenan 1962:172 and passim).

The nature of these contradictory political tendencies and their interrelationship can be explained by the historical context in which they arose. As the Catalan regionalist movement preceded and in fact retarded the growth of class conflict (Vilar 1962:I:154), I will discuss it first. The modern regionalist movement had its genesis in two discrete historical phenomena that appeared in the middle of the nineteenth century. The first was the effort on the part of the emergent bourgeoisie to gain political power commensurate with its economic strength. The second was a popular outburst of regionalist sentiment, sparked by a literary revival of Catalan folk culture known as the *Renaixença*. Both were directed toward mobilizing the Catalans against the central government, whose policies were considered responsible for the disastrous economic cycles in Catalonia (Brenan 1962:29).

The first manifestation of the bourgeoisie's drive for power took the form of a manufacturer's lobby, organized to pressure the central government to erect tariff barriers to protect Catalan industries. The manufacturers' association, the Industrial Institute of Catalonia,[17] was founded in 1844. Between that date and 1869, the institute secured high tariff policies from a series of nominally "free-trade" governments (Brenan 1962:27). When a genuine free-trade government came to power in 1869, the Catalan manufacturers sought to strengthen their political base by organizing a popular movement in which all Catalans could protest the prejudicial economic policies of Madrid.

The ideological component of this movement was drawn from a literary renaissance that had begun to flourish in metropolitan circles as early as 1828. As the industrial revolution sank roots in Catalonia, poets and essayists started to rediscover the Catalan literary tradition of the Middle Ages, and writings extolling the virtue of things Catalan began to appear (Brenan 1962:27–8). As an outgrowth of this literary tradition and cultural movement, popular voluntary associations sprang up to celebrate various aspects of Catalanism. In addition to literary associations, societies for practicing the *sardana* (the popular regional dance) and for mountain climbing appeared in provincial towns as well as in Barcelona. Though they served as emotional outlets for regionalist sentiments, the associations also owed their popularity to the fact that they were often the principal centers of recreation in small towns.

However, the principal florescence of these associations was after 1869, when members of the wealthy bourgeoisie became increasingly instrumental in their formation (Vicens Vives 1961:430–6). The bourgeoisie was first to conceive of the associations as political vehicles to forward its own interests, a tactic later used by a plethora of antibourgeoisie parties. While subsidizing these associations financially, the bourgeoisie made sure that among the cultural events glorified were institutions of economic utility, including the *rabassa morta* and related institutions in the countryside, and that the central government played the role of villain whenever economic woes beset the region (Brenan 1962:30).

The success of the bourgeoisie in rallying people of the Catalan cultural tradition to their banner through the associations can be seen from the massive electoral support accorded the first political party of the Catalan bourgeoisie. Known as the Regionalist League *(Lliga Regionalista)*, the party was formed in 1890 to compete in electoral politics with other regional and national political parties. Its program centered around Catalan autonomy, although within the framework of the central government. In 1907, this party, having organized diverse groups with regionalist sympathies into an electoral coalition called Catalan Solidarity *(Solidaridad*

Catalana), scored a smashing victory at the polls, electing forty-
one of its forty-four candidates to the Cortes (Brenan 1962:32; Carr
1966:549–51).

The success of the *lliga* indicates the widespread popular support
for the party throughout Catalonia and reflects upon the political
organization of the bourgeoisie itself. Support was achieved
through the cultural associations and the politics of *caciquismo*
(bossism). Prior to the elections the wealthy bourgeoisie of the *lliga*
sent political emissaries at local levels into action to mobilize the
vote in its favor. The emissaries were generally wealthy men who
held positions within the associations. By delivering the vote for
Solidaridad Catalana, these emissaries could promise some material favors to their constituents and could help them express their
regionalist fervor at the ballot box.

Despite the success of the *lliga* in the balloting of 1907, the
wealthy bourgeoisie soon abandoned the Catalan nationalist
movement it had worked so hard to create. Unfortunately, the
appeal of the Catalan nationalist movement was largely tied to the
notion of the perpetual prosperity of a permanently evolving
Catalonia, and this the party was unable to guarantee. Prosperity in
Catalonia had been cyclic throughout the nineteenth century
owing to market fluctuations, internal upheavals, and political
maneuvering by the state. The Achilles heel of bourgeois Catalan
nationalism was class conflict inflamed by the economic cycles.

Perhaps the most decisive factor in the abandonment of the
Catalan nationalist movement by the wealthy bourgeoisie was the
emergence of a revolutionary proletariat in Barcelona. The fatal
paradox of early Catalan nationalism was that although it was designed to unite people across the lines of social class, it had made
no provision to incorporate the manual laborers of Barcelona. As
the vast majority of the workers were of Castilian origin, they were
ideologically excluded from the movement (Brenan 1962:170 and
passim). As migrants from the miserable estates in the South, they
brought with them the peasant's rampant anarchism of that part of
the country, which now appeared as a religion of proletarianism
in the metropolis.

As early as the 1830s, workers' associations and movements had
been under sporadic repression. In 1909 in Barcelona the growing
conflict between workers and factory owners came to a head in
Tragic Week. Until the workers were put down by the army, the

city underwent nearly a week of anarchy and mob rule (Brenan 1962:34). From then on, despite occasional and inconsistent attempts to unify the workers under Catalanism (Vilar 1962:I:132 ff.), the Catalan bourgeoisie began to disentangle itself from the regionalist movement, seeking an accommodation with the Spanish state that would allow the national police and army to control the urban workers and unruly *rabassaires* in the countryside. The loss of political initiative by the Catalan haute bourgeoisie led it inexorably to support the military dictatorship of Primo de Rivera (1923–30) and, later, Franco's rise to power.[18]

3

Political economy of land tenure in the Alto Panadés

The present Catalan system of land tenure in viniculture districts, the *rabassa morta* contract, is the product of a process of economic colonization of the countryside initiated during the nineteenth century by the urban Catalan bourgeoisie.

General aspects of the "rabassa morta" contract

The juridical essentials of this form of contract originally were the following: (1) it was a long-term sharecropping contract based on the life of a vineyard, terminating after two-thirds of the original vines had died (prior to the 1880s, about fifty years; from the 1890s to the present, about twenty-five years); (2) shares of the harvest were one-third for the proprietor and two-thirds for the sharecropper *(rabassaire)*; no money changed hands, and it was incumbent upon both parties to produce wine independently of each other; and (3) in general, costs and methods of cultivation were in the hands of the sharecropper (Benach y Sonet 1911; Vilar 1962:II). In exceptional cases, tools and fertilizers might be provided by the proprietor, and in the case of a sharecropper who was also an overseer *(masover)*, it was incumbent upon the proprietor to provide lodging for the overseer's family. The only administrative check the proprietor maintained over production was the loosely held "code of the good peasant" *("us i costum de bon pagés")* that specified certain practices of cultivation (Giralt i Raventós 1964:56). The *rabassa morta* contract was designed to fix cultivators on the proprietor's land for a long period, to entrust the cultivator with all phases of cultivation, and to provide for the collection of rent in harvest.

The main incentive to colonization in the Catalan countryside was the wealth viniculture generated up to the 1880s, rather than the generosity of the *rabassa morta* contract. Oscillations in wine prices and/or crop conditions were then and are now a determining factor in relations between sharecropper and proprietor, although class conflict is an implicit and constant feature of the contract. In fact, in the nineteenth century, two main periods can be distinguished in the economic history of the *rabassa morta* system: a period before 1880 when wine prices were generally good, landlord-tenant relationships were relatively stable, and the institution of sharecropping governed by the contract flourished; and a period after 1880 when the loss of colonial markets, exacerbated by crop disaster, led to stagnation in wine prices and increasing conflict between *rabassaires* and proprietors. At present there is a strong possibility that this kind of sharecropping will disappear as the dominant mode of vinicultural exploitation.

The shift to vineyard cultivation in the nineteenth century had revolutionary overtones for the Alto Panadés, bringing about fundamental changes in labor, technology, and commerce. The rentier of vineyards replaced the large wheat cultivator as the economic cynosure of the district, just as the appearance of the *rabassaire* led to the extinction of the small rural proletariat that had cultivated the wheatfields. The main thrust of the metropolitan bourgeoisie and local gentry was directed initially toward the accumulation of forestland on the valley floor and slopes, and only gradually toward acquiring all arable land in the district. Owing partly to the labor requirements of land buying, this colonization resulted in the multitude of small holdings (averaging 2 to 3 hectares) that exist at present. At the same time, the immediate prosperity of vineyard permitted an enormous expansion in the amount of land under cultivation. From a district of relatively isolated wheat-growing estates and large forest tracts, the Alto Panadés became a treeless maze of small farms, interspersed with a few large properties.

The conversion of wheatfields to vineyard required a new technological order that also contributed to the tendency toward small holdings. Prior to the nineteenth century, agrarian technology remained medieval, characterized by shallow plowing, poorly executed broadcast sowing that tended to choke the wheat crop, little or no fertilization (with horse dung and straw), and a yearly fallow period (Giralt i Raventós 1958:11–12). Conversion to commercial viticulture meant the application of the best nineteenth-century technology, using metal plows, chemical fertilizers, and treatments against oidium and mildew employed to maximize pro-

duction for markets. New technological developments were most
notably diffused by the Institute of San Isidro, a voluntary association of large landowners dedicated to the improvements of crops,
wines, and market conditions throughout Catalonia (Vicens Vives
1961:192). Eventually, the interest in profit making by applying
new methods led to the foundation in 1901 of the Enology Station
in Vilafranca, which also served as mediator between commercial
interests and cultivators through its chemical analysis of alcoholic
gradations and impurities.

Despite technological change and consequent rationalization of
production, the basic elements of production – a man farming with
horse and plow – remained the same. While large wheat estates
worked by the casual methods of agriculture in use prior to the
nineteenth century required roughly one man for each 30 hectares,
viticulture required more labor. Vineyard needs constant care
(multiple plowings, fertilizing, and chemical treatments) from
March through September, and intermittent labor (planting, pruning of dead suckers, or removal of vines for fallow) from October
through February. Under these conditions, a man with horsedrawn plow could cultivate a maximum of 7 hectares of vineyard
each year. As the same man traditionally held a small plot (or plots)
1 or 2 hectares in size of garden land, 4 to 5 hectares of vineyard
became the average amount per sharecropper. In 1967 it was a
common arrangement for a sharecropper to own 2 or 3 hectares and
to work 4 or 5 hectares under *aparcería* or *rabassa morta* contracts
(Giró 1966:4).[1] Labor requirements for viticulture did not alone
determine the size of property holdings in the Alto Panadés; factors
such as price of land, physical contours of arable land, and the prior
existence of large estates contributed to a wide range in the size of
holdings, from less than 1 hectare to more than 1,000 hectares.
Though mean property size is currently about 3 hectares, which is
consistent with the dominance of sharecropping in the district
(Giró 1966:3), there has always been a substantial number of estates of over 30 hectares, principally located on the valley floor.

Lands marginal to wheat cultivation were quickly parceled out
into properties that could be worked by *rabassaires*, but many of
the old estates on the valley floor remained intact, either by simple
conversion to vineyard or by sale to wealthy speculators. The continued presence of these large estates contradicts the common por-
trayal of Catalonia as an area dominated by small holdings and

Size of agrarian properties in the Alto Panadés, 1966

	Size (hectares)					
	0.01–0.9	1.0–4.9	5.0–9.9	10.0–29.9	30.0–99.9	100–1,000
Number of properties[a]	812	2,997	1,531	297	210	71
Percent of total	13.1	51.2	25.7	5.0	3.6	1.4

Source: Giró 1966:3.

[a] These figures refer to the number of properties, not the number of owners of such properties; many men own more than one property.

sharecropped lands controlled by absentee owners (Brenan 1962:99). Such a characterization is correct in a numerical sense, but it obscures the fact that the large estates remained key pieces in the local economy and created a permanent local base for bourgeois political activity. Large proprietors usually had control of wine-producing facilities, merchandising, and transportation. By the 1870s some of the estates were the sites of the district's prominent wine companies, which purchased a large amount of wine produced by the *rabassaires* for subsequent elaboration and sale.

An example of the large estate, large business organization established in this period is the Cordorniu Champagnery. Using an original 180-hectare tract dating from 1554 as a base of operations, the Cordorniu built 10 miles of champagne caves between 1876 and 1900 (Mestre Artigas 1961:43–5). This company, like many others in the Alto Panadés, made its mark on the world market; it had sufficient market strength to single-handedly threaten contemporary French champagne vintners.[2] Cordorniu was scarcely an isolated example; various large estates spawned processing centers that had markets in Europe and the Americas, as well as in Catalonia and the Spanish interior.

The existence of relatively large estates was by no means peculiar to the Alto Panadés; it was a marked feature of all Catalan viticultural districts. Though the large estates constituted only 1 percent of cultivable land, they gave order to the gaggle of small parcels by providing a ready market for the *rabassaires'* grapes and wines, as well as an extra*comarcal* network for disposing of wine.

In contrast, the *productive mainstay* (as contrasted with the *commercial preeminence* of the large estate) was the small plot, whether owned by an absentee owner or an investing sharecropper.

To make the *rabassa morta* system operational, the speculator had to be able to offer advantageous conditions of colonization to the *rabassaire*. Foremost among the concessions was the term of tenure, which gave the *rabassaire* (de facto for his lifetime) a plot of land. Prior rental agreements in the district were all short-term, designed to give the owner a maximum amount of leverage over the lessee, reflecting the short-term lease vogue of the 1780s. Under the nineteenth-century *rabassa morta* contract, the tenure rights of the *rabassaire* were for about fifty years, the average life of a Catalan vineyard in the 1800s.[3]

In practice, the *rabassiare* could guarantee his tenure indefinitely, generally with the complicity of the proprietor. The means of achieving permanent tenure were simple: If the *rabassa morta* contract was based on the life of the vines, then the sharecropper would never allow the vines to die. As the vines began to enter the declining phase of their cycle (the last four years of the fifty-year cycle), the sharecropper resorted to the practice of *colgats*.[4] To make a *colgat*, the *rabassaire* would double-over a sucker from a living vine into the space left by the removal of a dead neighboring vine, thus causing a new vine to grow in place of the old. Thus, the vineyard never died, and the sharecropper hypothetically never had to negotiate a new contract. *Colgats* initially benefited the proprietor because the practice increased the yield of the vineyard, consequently increasing the landlord's profits (Giralt i Raventós 1964:57). This practice became the principal cause of the juridical ambiguities surrounding the *rabassa morta* contract when the tenancy problem acquired political dimensions.[5]

In addition to long-term tenure and administrative rights over agricultural procedures, the proprietors conceded advantageous shares to the *rabassaire* in the division of the harvest. Shares were generally two-thirds for the sharecropper and one-third for the proprietor, with the stipulation that fruits be drawn from all sections of the vineyard to ensure that good and bad vines were shared by both. Sharecropping did not apply to vineyard only, but to all crops grown for commercial purposes, with shares based on the profitability of the crop in question. The more profitable the crop, the greater the share of the proprietor. In the case of wheat, the second most important crop of the district and the one used as vineyard fallow, the shares were and still are four-fifths for the sharecropper and one-fifth for the owner. Even garden crops entered into shares; garlics, for example, were split ten to one in favor of the sharecropper.

In the growing agricultural prosperity of the nineteenth century, sharecropping was deemed advantageous because sufficient profit could be made on it to provide the sharecropper with investment capital (for land and/or small wealth and familial mobility). To such settlers, the Alto Panadés was especially attractive after the introduction of champagne grapes, because its soil was ideal for high-yield vines, producing three to four times the volume of neighboring viticulture districts.

Landlord-"rabassaire" relations prior to 1939

The dynamics of the *rabassa morta* system lay not so much in its juridical formulation as in the commercial atmosphere surrounding the contract. Agricultural wealth came, not from the grapes produced in the fields, but from the wines that had to be elaborated and sold on the open market. The colonization of the land was accompanied by a growth in the middle 1850s of wine-related commerce, warehouses, pressing centers, cart and barrel industries, and transportation facilities (roads, shipping, railroad). Heavily invested in by the metropolitan bourgeoisie, these provided an entirely new commercial network for the district (Giralt i Raventós 1958:162). Thus the sharecropper was thrust into the market and forced to cope with all its alternatives and allocative choices. His response was to commercialize his own production, to plant every square centimeter of his land with some salable item. The *rabassaire* might grow wheat, cultivate a garden, and raise rabbits and chickens near his dwelling; yet he was never able to feed his own family entirely on what he produced. Equipped with some of the elements of self-sufficiency, he found it more profitable to cultivate for profit and to buy some staples on the open market.

This entrepreneurial orientation was not simply the result of immersion in a market context. It was by conscious design on the part of the metropolitan bourgeoisie that the *rabassa morta* system, rather than a wage-labor contract, was instituted. One might ask, especially in view of the conflicts that eventually surrounded the *rabassa morta* contract, why the *rabassaires* were not offered annual contracts on a wage-labor basis or in terms of some contractual formula other than *rabassa morta*. To attempt to answer this question, we must refer to the political atmosphere of the nineteenth century.

Chapter 2 has indicated that the industrial development of Catalonia in the nineteenth century involved the urban bourgeoisie in two kinds of conflicts: class conflict with the proletariat and political conflict with the state. Owing to the conflict with the Spanish state, the metropolitan bourgeoisie was unable to depend on the support of the national police forces monopolized by the state in pressing its claims in the class conflict. Under these circumstances the growing proletariat became a tremendous threat to the metropolitan bourgeoisie, and urban Catalonia until 1939 was plagued by nearly unprecedented labor turbulence (Brenan 1962:131–202).

Given the dynamic but precarious position of the Catalan bourgeoisie, it is not surprising that the *rabassa morta* contract was conceived as a political as well as an economic institution. The bourgeoisie effectively anticipated the dangers of placing workers under annual contract in control of vineyards whose owners were quite often absent. A long-term agreement extended in the context of a prospering market gave the *rabassaire* an appealing stake in the new society being propagated by the urban bourgeoisie. In contrast to the miserable wages of the unskilled proletariat, a *rabassaire* had a great deal of influence over his own earnings and consequently more latitude in life horizons than did the man who settled in Barcelona's celebrated proletarian ghetto, the *Barrio Chino*. The chief virtue of the *rabassa morta* contract, as Giralt i Raventós (1958:18) has pointed out, was to "avoid the proletarianization of the countryside."

The importance of social mobility in nineteenth-century Catalonia cannot be overstressed, especially in connection with the aspirations of the *rabassaires*. Mobility was not simply something that might happen to a person who chose to be a *rabassaire;* it was a social doctrine, a part of the ideology surrounding the development of the region. In the countryside, the ideology of mobility even acquired a name, *pairalisme* (allegiance to paternal house), a doctrine delineating the step-by-step path of individual advance. In essence, *pairalisme* stressed the dynamic nature of the Catalan *hereu-pubilla* inheritance system, which allotted all fixed assets acquired by a father to the firstborn son, or failing a son, to the firstborn daughter.

Yet the social meaning of *pairalisme* was not that of simple primogeniture. It was clearly understood that the firstborn child should administer the fixed assets of the father to capitalize the business enterprises of his younger siblings (Maspons i Anglasells 1935:176), that he should provide business or professional backing for his brothers or arrange advantageous marriages for his sisters. Mobility was thus a familial, as opposed to an individual, matter; the key to success lay first in acquiring land and then in administering it while offspring moved upward into strategic niches within *comarcal* society. Giralt i Raventós (1964:54) warns however, that "one must distrust the *pairalist* view of the rural world, and its bucolic image disseminated by drawing room agronomists since the *Renaixença.*"

On arrival in any district, the *rabassaire* was, of course, without land; sharecropping did not entitle him to ownership. His primary goals were to stabilize his sharecropped land by the practice of *colgats* and to attempt to purchase land on his own. His ability to buy land generally depended on the business failures of his neighbors, common enough so that most *rabassaires* had in the course of a lifetime at least one opportunity to buy a couple of hectares from a neighboring proprietor. The best source of land was another *rabassaire* who suddenly found himself in dire straits and was forced to sell his own small tract to cancel debts. Both large owners and speculators could more easily weather a crop failure or a downturn of wine prices than a *rabassaire*, as they had more liquid assets and were backstopped by investments in other economic sectors. Hence, they did not have to sell portions of their holdings to keep out of debt. The competition for land among *rabassaires*, each awaiting his neighbor's failure, must have accentuated each man's drive for mobility as well as for survival.

Although the ideological underpinnings of *rabassa morta* and *pairalisme* stressed the accomplishments of the individual, the sharecropper also realized that his goals could be achieved most easily by developing favorable relations with an owner. A large landowner had extensive contacts with Vilafranca and elsewhere and could use such contacts to help place the younger son of a favored *rabassaire* in a suitable occupation. He could help the *rabassaire* with loans to tide him over a bad year, subsidize the *rabassaire's* investment, tip him off to a good business venture, and indicate the appropriate person to aid him in legal difficulties.

To gain favored status with the owner was a sharecropper's continuous preoccupation. Appropriate social tactics might eventually allow him to occupy the strategic social position of *masover*. Legally, all that differentiated the *masover* from an ordinary *rabassaire* was the concession of lodging, but the relationship was much more productive for the *masover* than the de jure structure would indicate. In addition to his loyalty as an overseer, a *masover* was selected for his technical competence in viticulture and his ability to make shrewd commerical judgments, talents he could exercise in the absentee owner's behalf. By rising to the position of *masover*, a man could put himself in a better position to receive both material benefits and strategic information for himself. There was also the possibility that an owner might sell him a small plot, both to ensure his goodwill and to fix him in the immediate area of the owner's property. *Masoveria* was, then, one of the dynamic institutions of the viticultural revolution: It guaranteed the owner's interest even though he retained only indirect control of the productive process (Vicens Vives 1961:84), and it constituted one more rung on the ladder of mobility for the *rabassaire*.

The success of the *rabassa morta* system in developing the countryside in an atmosphere of relatively stable class relations until the 1880s has been remarked by various scholars (Vicens Vives 1959:98; Giralt i Raventós 1964:12). In fact, *pairalist* writers insist that the *rabassaire*-landlord conflict that broke out in the 1880s was fomented by outside agitators (see Giralt i Raventós 1964:45–55). However, the conflict clearly manifested itself before the overt politicization of the countryside in the last decades of the nineteenth century, as a result of the very success of the *rabassa morta* system in giving the *rabassaire* entrepreneurial goals. To be sure, the *rabassaire* devoted his life to self-advancement, but self-advancement was viewed as stemming from the independent possession of land. Not only was the *rabassa morta* system a block to his acquisition of land, but the owner, who expended little or no effort, claimed part of the harvest and diminished the *rabassaire's* liquid wealth. Thus, while the *rabassa morta* system fired the aspirations of the *rabassaire*, it also thwarted them. The sharecropper came to view the owner as a parasite; his battle cry became: "The land for he who tills it."

Initially, the conflict took place in a juridical context between individual owners and individual *rabassaires* around the issue of whether the practice of *colgats* constituted a de jure renewal of the *rabassa morta* contract (Benach y Sonet 1911:27). Implicit in this legal question was a basic socioeconomic one: Could the *rabassaire*, through the practice of *colgats*, ensure himself de facto perpetual tenure in a vineyard? Catalan jurisprudence was vague on this point; there were conflicting laws on ownership that indicated, on the one hand, ownership by usufruct and, on the other hand, ownership by possession of title. This uncertainty allowed the *rabassaire* to argue that "the *rabassa morta* constituted a property tax and the *rabassaire* (usufruct) could redeem the rights of ownership (direct ownership) with the capitalization of the shares of fruits which were the basis of the tax" (Mas i Perera 1932:78; Giralt i Raventós 1964:56).

Rulings on such cases, which began to appear regularly by the 1860s, were complicated by contradictions. The supreme tribunal of the region was quite conscious of the danger of class conflict in the Catalan countryside and its potential in checking the nationalist goals of the Catalan metropolitan bourgeoisie. However, representing the metropolitan bourgeoisie, the tribunal was equally conscious of the sanctity of property. The proprietors themselves contributed to the difficult task of establishing clear legal judgments both by permitting *colgats* and by generally failing to file public records of the *rabassa morta* contract.

Colgats, as mentioned above, were economically beneficial to both owner and sharecropper; yet they sometimes became a means of dispossessing the proprietor who condoned them. Reliance on verbal rather than written contracts posed more serious problems. Public records were exorbitantly priced, and the contracts made between each proprietor and *rabassaire* were personal and somewhat elastic. Benach y Sonet (1911:23) states that "*rabassaires* and proprietors in the Panadés have never suspected that in order to create an agreement of first fruits that it was necessary to do more than mutually agree on the methods of cultivation of the soil and the quota of fruits due the proprietor."

Emphasizing the individual nature of these contracts somewhat obscures the owner's basic reason for not making a public contract.

In order to settle court cases between *rabassaires* and proprietors, the tribunal had to discover the actual number of annual payments in fruit that the owner had received from the sharecropper. If these exceeded fifty (approximately the life of a vineyard prior to the 1880s), then the contract might be construed to have been renewed by both parties. Records of both contract agreements and profits were usually recorded in a tax ledger, which was maintained by the proprietor and was not a public document. These records were not public documents because of "the desire of the proprietors to avoid creating by means of a public document a valid title of property rights to the land in the *rabassaires'* favor" (Giralt i Raventós 1964:59–60).

Prior to the destruction of the vines by phylloxera, and despite almost a century's juridical conflict over the matter, "the divorce between ownership and usufruct was so clear . . . that the *rabassa* land was inscribed in the *rabassaire's* name in the mortgage register and property registers, as though he were the real proprietor" (Giralt i Raventós 1964:56). The land appeared in *rabassaires'* inheritance inventories, and only the shares appeared in the owners' inheritance inventories. By refusing to register publicly his rental contracts, the owner thus hid in a private transcript what might have condemned him before the public tribunal.

Because of such juridical ambiguities, as well as the political situation in Catalonia at the time, it was predictable that test cases before the Catalan tribunal would have inconclusive results. Of two test cases from the Alto Panadés in 1865, one resulted in the transfer of land from the proprietor (whose family had purchased it 109 years prior to the suit) to the *rabassaire;* the other allowed the proprietor to expel the *rabassaire* from land the latter's family had cultivated for three generations (Benach y Sonet 1911:27). In both cases, the practice of *colgats* was involved. The decisive point in each case was whether the proprietor had given tacit consent to *colgats* or whether the *rabassaire* had proceeded strictly on his own initiative. In the Alto Panadés, and probably most other districts, tacit complicity of the proprietor was obvious if the owner lived in the district and was in question only in cases involving absentee owners (Benach y Sonet 1911:32). Threatened by the possibility of losing their land through the juridical process, the owners again pressed the tribunal to prohibit *colgats*, which it did in 1883. Under this decision, the *rabassaire* was required to commit the economic absurdity of allowing the vineyards to die (Giralt i Raventós 1964:57).

However, this judgment by no means terminated the juridical ambiguities of the *rabassa morta* contract. For the owner to prove the existence of *colgats*, the tax ledger had to be given the status of a public document so that the law could judge the strength of the *rabassaire's* claim. The net result of this confusion was a plethora of lawsuits by sharecroppers against proprietors that lasted from the 1860s until the late 1950s. Because of the enormous number of cases and their individual complexities, these suits tended to continue indefinitely. However, although the owner-*rabassaire* lawsuits were common, they were still individual contests over tenure rights, as contrasted with political struggles between classes, which were soon to follow.

The development of political organizations in the Alto Panadés in part grew out of the tenure struggle; its roots were in the 1880s when economic conditions in the district began to deteriorate. Ironically, this was precisely the moment when the Catalan movement began to gain momentum under the direction of the metropolitan bourgeoisie. These simultaneous developments no doubt account for many of the ensuing political ambiguities in the position of the *rabassaires* as the politicization of Catalonia proceeded.

The crisis in local viticulture was precipitated by a general fall in market prices for local wines. In part, falling wine prices were a direct consequence of the efficiency of *rabassa morta* colonization in the district; there was an overabundance of Panadés wine on the market because every available plot in the district was under cultivation and more wine was produced than consumed. Adding to the problem of overproduction was the competition of wines from other districts. Owing perhaps to early success with individual wine production and subsequent mixtures developed by private companies, cultivators in the Alto Panadés generally ignored cooperativism and other methods that would have improved the quality of their wines.[6] Consequently, districts that upgraded their wines gained a competitive advantage over the Alto Panadés (Vidal Barraguer, 1966:38–9).

It took a natural disaster to provide the impetus for the first coalitions of *rabassaires* in the district. This was the phylloxera (vine-louse) plague, which destroyed all vineyards in the decade 1890–1900. If the drop in wine prices made the economic situation of the sharecropper difficult by curbing his ability to accumulate capital, the vine-louse plague reduced him to near subsistence gardening until vineyards could be restored in the early 1900s. In addition, because the vineyards died, some landlords held to the letter of the *rabassa morta* contract and evicted their tenants; thus "the ancient discussion on the legality of *colgats* ceased because all the vines died, whether they were young or old or renewed or not" (Giralt i Raventós 1964:60). The exigencies of replanting and the need for labor led to the formulation of a new contract, based on the life of the new vines.

Despite a bleak economic and juridical situation, there was no mass migration of sharecroppers from the district, nor were the *rabassaires* reduced to starvation. Most of them simply awaited the restoration of vineyard, guaranteed by the previously successful French experience following vine-louse infestation. Although the plague infected the district for over a decade, few sharecroppers' fields were without vineyard for its duration. The vine louse spread gradually, and blighted fields were replanted by the crossing of the louse-resistant North American *Vinis rupestris* with local stocks. Thus a *rabassaire* commonly lost about four or five years' crops, one year's crop to plague and three or four years' crops waiting for new vine to bear fruit.

Although vineyards were replaced rapidly, the landlords showed no inclination to provide any kind of economic relief to the sharecroppers. Faced with substantial losses of revenue themselves, they attempted to recoup some of these losses by insisting upon receiving shares of the garden crops raised in the blighted fields. This practice sharpened the misery of the *rabassaire,* and the need to cross local vines with American stock aggravated the remaining juridical conflict over tenure rights. This was so because the adoption of *Vinis rupestris* meant that the viticulture cycle (without the practice of *colgats*) was shortened to twenty-five years from the fifty years the European *Vinis viniferis* had allowed. Within a sharecropper's lifetime, his tenancy might have to be renegotiated. In response to these twin catastrophes of economic disaster and dwindling contractual security, the first local peasant associations (sharecropper defense leagues) in the Alto Panadés were reported in 1890, 1892, and 1895 (Mas i Perera 1932:79).

Little is known of the salient organizational features of these early *rabassaire* associations. Mas i Perera (1932:79–80), the most reliable chronicler of this era, provides scant information about the ideology, leadership, and activities of these primitive defense leagues. His account makes clear, however, that the defense leagues were confined to single villages (rather than the *comarca*) and that their aims were to redeem or seize large properties. Their tactics generally consisted of refusing the owner his share of the crop and threatening physical reprisals against large proprietors.[7]

These early defense leagues lacked sufficient power to wrest control of lands from the large proprietors, but their appearance added a new dimension to the political structure of the *comarca*. From this time on, the *rabassaires* had to be considered as a potentially independent political force in their own right. During the early phases of the colonization, the *rabassaires* were politically an agglomeration of individuals. By 1890, common suffering began to foster the rudiments of class consciousness and political organization along class lines. Through the next thirty years, the *rabassaires* slowly evolved as a political class until, in 1928, the *rabassaires* of the Alto Panadés entered the Pan-Catalan Peasant League.

The *rabassaires'* political trajectory toward radicalism was neither linear nor free from contradictions. Rather, it proceeded in fits and starts amid a fog of political ambiguity. Until the civil war, the *rabassaires* of the Alto Panadés showed as much interest in reaching compromise settlements with large proprietors as they did in seizing their lands. Oscillations in political loyalties occurred as economic fortunes of the *rabassaires* rose or fell, as they were courted or rebuffed by the proprietors and as coalitions with various parties succeeded or failed. In spite of these vacillations, however, each time the *rabassaires* suffered political or economic reversals under whatever alliance prevailed at the moment, they emerged more organized and more radical.

An exposition on the nature of political alliances in the *comarca* is attempted in Chapter 4; here, one example of this vacillation may help clarify the above analysis of *rabassaire* politics. Even during their most radical phase (1928–39), the *rabassaires* in the Alto Panadés did not forsake the ideological framework of Catalan nationalism. Whatever coalitions they entered into were confined to Catalonia; never did the *rabassaires* of the district form long-term coalitions with the political parties originating from other regions of the country, regardless of their national or class pretensions. The paradox in this refusal of the *rabassaires* to forsake Catalan nationalism in favor of alliance with some of the Centrist and anti-Catalan parties is obvious: From 1890 to 1910, Catalan nationalism was sparked by the metropolitan bourgeoisie. Conversely, the anti-Catalan sentiments of the parties from other parts of Spain were antibourgeoisie as much as anti-Catalan. Thus the *rabassaires* forged their defense leagues of this era while remaining fundamentally within the political orbit of the Catalan bourgeoisie, who were the chief targets of the defense leagues.

This paradox can be explained by the political and economic complexities in the *comarca* and in Catalonia. On one hand, the *rabassaires* could only agree with the Catalan Nationalists that the Spanish state (and the Centrist parties clustered around it) were blocking the material progress of Catalonia. Many of the *rabassaires'* economic problems appeared to stem from the disastrous war of 1898. In this conflict with the United States, Spain had lost Cuba and the Philippines, prime wine markets for Catalan wine growers. The metropolitan bourgeoisie dwelt constantly on the damage to the interests of Catalonia that resulted from this war, including the damage to the wine market (Brenan 1962:31). On the other hand, and more importantly, the *rabassaires* could identify with many of the goals of the Catalan haute bourgeoisie. Quite apart from the spirit of Catalan regionalism, concrete economic and social issues linked the interests of the *rabassaires* to those of the bourgeoisie and its local expression, the large proprietors. The life goals of the *rabassaires* were predicated on entrepreneurial talents, just as were those of the large proprietors. Many of the *rabassaires* appear to have felt that there could be some accommodation of interests among like-minded people.

The large proprietors, for their part, sought to prevent the politicization of the *rabassaires* through technological improvement of viniculture. The decisive feature in maintaining the sharecroppers' political loyalty may have been the spectacular effort made by the owners to improve and commercialize viniculture to shore up the economic fortunes of the sharecroppers. The establishment in 1901 of the Enology Station in Vilafranca del Panadés is the most significant example. This institution was devoted to research on quality of stocks, dissemination of a new agricultural technique, and settling disputes between buyers and sellers over the chemical content of wines. The efforts of the station and of the

Agrarian Institute of San Isidro helped stabilize wine prices and relieve the economic want of the sharecropper. Development of champagneries was also furthered, aiding some cultivators. And when World War I broke out in 1914, prices for all Spanish wines soared on the world market. This produced temporary prosperity and rekindled the faith of the *rabassaires* in their ability to prosper under existing arrangements. It seemed then as if the tenancy dispute could continue forever without the total alienation of the *rabassaires* from their landlords.

Given the possibilities of an understanding between the large proprietors and the *rabassaires* in which each would benefit the other economically, it is not surprising that the *rabassaires* aided the proprietors in their Catalanist electoral politics. In the Alto Panadés *caciquismo* dominated by the proprietors remained the supreme politics until 1923, when the dictatorship of Primo de Rivera took power. Under this dictatorship, the Catalan bourgeoisie was provided the services of the state police, which added a new dimension to Catalan politics. In Barcelona, the police force was mobilized against the revolutionary proletariat. In the countryside, similar developments were not long in coming.

In the Alto Panadés, the accession of the Primo regime provided a signal for the owners to initiate the eviction of quarrelsome tenants, including those with pending lawsuits and those with uncomfortable political tendencies. This was done simply by stating that a contract had terminated and by bringing in the police to remove the *rabassaire* from his home if he persisted. In their attempts to localize politically dissident *rabassaires*, the owners also enlisted the services of a section of the clergy, referred to as *beneficiados*. The *beneficiado* was a priest who was supported by a wealthy person to do works for the faith. A large estate often had a private chapel where the *beneficiado* said mass exclusively for the proprietor's family. A further duty of the *beneficiado* was to visit the sharecroppers and report back to the landowner about the *rabassaire's* political adherence, his opinion of the proprietor, and moral qualities. This spy system led to the expulsion of many sharecroppers from their lands. It also turned the *rabassaires* into the ferocious anticlericalists they remain at present.

During the repression of the Primo regime (1923–30), the *rabassaires* of the Alto Panadés became increasingly radical in their political activities. Apart from developing ties with popular Catalan political parties, the sharecroppers began to seize the initiative in dealing with the economic crisis that had again affected viniculture areas. Their economic actions centered around the development of viniculture cooperatives in the Alto Panadés. The economic goals of the cooperatives were simple: By centralizing viniculture, the quality of ordinary table wine would improve, and consequently, wine would fetch a higher price on the open market. But economic issues were only one side of cooperativism (Campllonch 1917). Village cooperatives in Catalonia were products of the class struggle between landlords and sharecroppers and were local centers of *rabassaire* political resistance to local proprietors. Through the cooperatives, strikes and boycotts against the owners were organized. Strikes took the form of leaving some of the owners' fields uncultivated; boycotts prevented processing the owners' shares of the grape harvest at the cooperative (Giralt i Raventós 1964:65). Both methods, as well as the threat of physical reprisal, were *rabassaire* responses to the machinations of the large proprietors.

In addition to serving political and economic needs of the *rabassaires*, the cooperatives were often social centers. In the Campo de Tarragona, the center of the cooperative movement, the cooperatives established mutual benefit funds, held dances and other entertainment, frequently hired their own doctor, and sometimes established schools for the *rabassaires*' children.[8] In the Alto Panadés, the pattern was much the same, although the cooperatives were less radical than those of the Campo de Tarragona[9] and emphasized economic issues, such as raising wine prices, rather than expropriation of the landlords. The conservativism of the *rabassaires* of the Alto Panadés, reflected in the cooperative movement, stands in contrast to the radicalism of the sharecroppers of the Campo de Tarragona. In the latter region, cooperativism began at the end of the nineteenth century[10] and by 1920 had reached a stage in which *rabassaires* and large proprietors had competing viniculture cooperatives, often in the same village. None of the cooperatives in the Alto Panadés prompted formation of countercooperatives by large proprietors. Most villages in this district appear to have eschewed cooperativism in favor of individual economic independence. The weakness of the cooperative movement in the Alto Panadés has been attributed by various local *rabassaires* to the wealth of the district during optimum market conditions. Yield from the local vines is two to three times higher than that in other viticultural districts, and the relative wealth of the Alto Panadés, my informants argued, made the sharecroppers more disposed to economic individualism than their counterparts in the poorer districts of the Campo de Tarragona.

Despite the weakness of the cooperative movement in the Alto Panadés, the *rabassaires* were not inactive in other types of political organizations. In a mass meeting in Vilafranca in 1928, 'the sharecroppers voted to join the Pan-Catalan Peasant League. The league's main organizing force came from the Campo de Tarragona cooperativists, and its programs were those of the village cooperativists. Yet even in the midst of the revolutionary excitement, the sharecroppers remained ambivalent toward the large proprietors. A number of *rabassaires* refused to join the league and continued to hope for improvement in landlord-tenant relationships under the *rabassa morta* contract. These *rabassaires*, referred to by league members as *esquirols* (scabs), were subjected to beatings and fines by league sharecroppers. Even the *rabassaires* who joined the league showed ambivalence toward the large proprietors. A proprietor was never shot by a sharecropper who lived in the same village; *rabassaire* liquidation squads always operated outside their own village.[11] Apparently the sharecroppers could not bring themselves to kill men with whom they had personal relationships, no matter how miserable these relationships were.

Expropriation of the vineyards by the *rabassaires* did not lead to the spread of cooperativism during the civil war (1936–9). In sharecropper radicalism the Alto Panadés lagged far behind the viticulture districts of the Campo de Tarragona. Each *rabassaire* simply had a little more land after the division and distribution of the large owners' properties, and his wealth was further enhanced by his monopoly on all the fruits of his lands. Under these conditions, *rabassaire* economic individualism flourished until the triumph of the Franco forces in 1939 restored the lands to the surviving proprietors or their descendants.

Impact of the Franco regime on the tenancy dispute

More than three decades since the beginning of the Franco regime, the viticultural economy of the Alto Panadés remains in crisis. However, the district is moving from nearly total dependence on viticulture to reliance on the growth of light industry as a supplement to revenue from viticulture. Viticulture itself is being reorganized both technologically and in terms of the social organization of production. This reorganization has been made possible by the introduction of farm machinery into the vineyards. Since 1956, machines have progressively replaced the *rabassaire* as the chief instrument of production in the vineyards. But the rate of mechanization is so gradual as to be almost imperceptible. The Alto Panadés still resembles a classical Catalan viniculture district, in which sharecropping is dominant. Some 85 percent of the vineyards are still worked by sharecroppers; mechanization affects less than 1 hectare in 30 (Giró 1966:4). There are only 489 tractors in the entire district and only an infinitesimal number of properties is completely mechanized.[12] Progress in improving the quality of table wines has also been painfully slow. Although it has been known for some time that cooperativism would improve the quality of basic stocks, the first substantial cooperative since the Primo era was completed only in 1966.

The slow pace of agrarian transformation is caused only in part by the district's economic structure; a more important factor is the continuing complexity of relationships among landlords, tenants, and the state. The Franco regime dynamically intervened in the economy of the Alto Panadés in the form of agrarian credits and agrarian legislation related to mechanization. The regime's impact has been felt in all the critical aspects of the viticulture crisis. Through economic policy and attendant social legislation, the central government has become the principal agent of modernization in the Alto Panadés. It has replaced the large proprietor as the dominant economic force in the *comarca*.

To explain the role of the Franco regime in the agrarian transformation of the Alto Panadés and its effects on landlords and tenants, it is necessary to outline the present crisis in viticulture. The crisis hinges on the falling value of the district's ordinary wines. In spite of the district's fame as the champagne center of Spain, only 7 percent of the 1965 grape crop was utilized for champagne (Giró 1966:6). The mainstay of the region's viniculture is ordinary white wine, produced by each cultivator as he sees fit. Owing to the complexities of wine elaboration, these products are generally of inferior quality. Because of advances in other viniculture districts, notably in the adoption of cooperativism, the ordinary wine of the Alto Panadés has had an increasingly difficult time maintaining its price in the open market. Despite successive devaluations of the peseta, wine prices in the district have remained almost constant at 32 pesetas per percent alcohol per hectoliter and would have declined had not a state subsidy established in 1963 maintained that price level.

Until recently the system of individual wine production allowed wide latitude for errors in elaboration. If errors were so drastic that the brew was unacceptable as wine, it could be sold as commercial alcohol. Although less profitable than wine, such sales allowed the producer to recoup some of his losses. However, the development of transport facilities has allowed the diffusion of cheaper industrial alcohols, thus undercutting the market for vinicultural alcohol (Giralt i Raventós 1966:19). Today almost all the ordinary wine that reaches the market is sold to one of the district's wineries, each of which employs a chemist whose job is to work enough magic by blending to produce a salable product. Some of the wineries produce respectable wines; but brews that no amount of chemical magic can retrieve are sold anonymously to proprietors of cheap taverns. These tavernkeepers reputedly work still further magic on the wines; watering is said to be a common practice, and until recently blue vitriol was sometimes added to watered wine to give it some punch. These malpractices further cheapen the value of ordinary wine, reinforcing the viniculture crisis.

Resolution of the crisis depends on eliminating individual wine production and concentrating wine making in a champagnery or cooperative that can handle all facets of elaboration and commercialization. Yet concentration presents different alternatives to large owners than to *rabassaires*. Some owners can raise profits by adopting mechanization, which displaces the *rabassaires* and allows the owner to take the sharecropper's portion of the harvest. But improvement in cultivation alone does not lead to higher wine prices; improvement in elaboration is necessary as well. Therefore, owners must either initiate their own elaboration centers or support cooperativism. As joining a cooperative involves less personal risk, this is the route to prosperity preferred by large proprietors. For the sharecroppers, on the other hand, the cooperative is the only answer to survival in viniculture.

To mechanize his holdings, a large proprietor must first control his lands administratively. He must be able to demonstrate clear title of ownership and show that he is not bound to the tenant by a long-term contract of the *rabassa morta* type. The juridical vehicle for demonstrating lack of contractual obligation to the sharecropper is the *aparcería*, a sharecropping contract like the *rabassa morta*, but for one year only. If the proprietor wishes to push his tenants off his properties and can demonstrate that he has this type of contract with them, the tenants must move. Because *aparcería* contracts are often verbal, as were many of the *rabassa morta* contracts, the same juridical disputes and lawsuits arise as were associated with the earlier contracts. In any case, a proprietor cannot simply expel a sharecropper from his holdings when the contract expires. He is required by the state to pay the sharecropper for the value of the crops on the land and to reimburse him for improvements made upon the property. This compensation, referred to as "improvements," is strictly adhered to by the proprietors. If proprietor and tenant do not agree upon the value of the improvements, this value is determined by an official of the state, an agrarian surveyor, whose assessment is binding on both parties. The value of the required compensation varies according to the quality and location of the land, as well as the improvements it has undergone; the mean value per hectare in 1967 was approximately 60,000 pesetas ($1,000).[13] Although this price is high enough to slow the process of eviction of tenants, such evictions take place with increasing frequency each year. The large proprietors cannot afford to purchase land on the open market; competitors from industry and tourism are willing to pay double this tenant-compensation value for agrarian properties.[14] Thus owners are forced to redeem land to which they already hold title, a process that often takes years for completion.

Besides compensation payments to the *rabassaires*, the proprietors must bear the cost of machinery and must have enough contiguous property to profit by mechanization. It has been estimated that the cost of completely mechanizing a 20-hectare estate is approximately 720,000 pesetas ($12,000); a 20-hectare estate is considered the minimum property holding that will profit from mechanization (Giró 1966:6). The fact that fewer than 300 of the nearly 6,000 agrarian properties in the Alto Panadés are 20 hectares or larger explains why mechanization of the district's vineyards is still uncommon.

Few large proprietors have (or are disposed to spend) the capital necessary for mechanization of their estates; many must turn to the

Agrarian Credit Bank for cash loans. If a landholder accepts a state loan, he must do so under the terms of the Agrarian Credit Law of 1954.[15] The cardinal tenet of this law is that agrarian credits can be granted only for further cultivation carried out by the owner of the property. The proprietor who receives state credits must carry out both redemption of property and mechanization under his own administration. The state allows six years from the date the loan was granted for redemption and mechanization. Should the proprietor fail in his undertaking, or violate the self-administration section of the law, he stands to forfeit his property. Thus the large landowner faces a double dilemma. Under present conditions, viticulture yields low profits; mechanization is, therefore, desirable and credits to finance it necessary. But to obtain the credits from the state, the proprietor, long a rentier whose knowledge of viticulture is limited to its commercial aspects, must actually learn to farm.

The large proprietors have evolved several strategies to cope with this dilemma. The one most used at present is to surround themselves with hired technicians familiar with various aspects of agriculture and agrarian technology. These technicians fall into two categories: the few hired laborers who tend the vineyards (under the owner's watchful eye, of course) and technical consultants, men who understand the relationship of machines to vineyards. The hired laborers are usually sons of *rabassaires* from the immediate neighborhood. They are paid wages competitive with those paid in industry, about 200 pesetas ($3.30) daily for an experienced hand. The consultants are government service personnel (from the Agrarian Extension Service, for example), mechanics, machinery salesmen, and the like. There is a sprinkling of this type of personnel throughout the *comarca*, but their heaviest concentration is in Vilafranca. Although they generally receive some cash for their services, their relationship with the large proprietors far transcends the cash aspect. Such people are in scarce supply and sorely needed; they are generally courted by the proprietors and frequently enter into patron-client relationships with them, as is discussed in Chapter 5.

A potential strategy of the large proprietor engaged in the modernization of his estate is to educate one or more of his sons in the methods of agriculture. Although agriculture as a profession is almost unknown among landlords,[16] several of those I interviewed

Loading barrels of wine at the end of harvest

had sons studying to become either agrarian engineers or agrarian surveyors. Either of these professions produces an heir capable of overseeing the family estate in all respects, a talent the father does not now possess.

Even if all the tracts suitable for mechanization could be modernized in the near future, the problem of raising wine prices would not be solved. It costs more per hectare to maintain a mechanized estate than one worked by *rabassaires*.[17] *Rabassaires*, after all, receive no salary and their use enables the owner to avoid the cost of machines. Also, neither yield nor quality of the grapes necessarily improves under mechanization. It is thus not surprising that the owners are the principal supporters and prime movers in the cooperative movement, although they have had difficulty adopting cooperative principles.

A few years before the cooperative was established in 1966 with state credit, twenty large owners attempted to set up their own cooperative, with emphasis on product commercialization rather than elaboration. However, most of the twenty sent only their worst wines to the cooperative, saving their best stock for the open market. The venture failed after two years. Yet three of the as-

Unloading grapes at the viniculture cooperative

sociates immediately petitioned the central government for state funds to establish a large-scale cooperative. Their request was vetoed by the labor minister of the provincial government, through which it had to be channeled. However, the cooperative's president-elect was well connected in Madrid; the veto was forgotten and a credit of 60 million pesetas granted in 1965.[18]

This credit, however, was subject to formidable conditions set down by the state. The 60-million peseta loan had to be guaranteed by the liquid capital of the prospective directorate; should the cooperative fail, the state would have a lien on the bank accounts of the directorate members for the full amount of the loan. Furthermore, the cooperative was to be open to all cultivators in the district, on a first-come, first-served basis, large owners and *rabassaires* together. In addition, the directorate could not constitute a permanent board of directors, but was subject to replacement by vote of the members. The directorate agreed to these conditions and began to enlist 600 members for the fall 1966 harvest and to construct two branches of the cooperative. Organization was begun by calling an informal council of large holders with an interest in joining the cooperative. This informal alliance along kin and class lines then laid the basis for organization at the village level, using the estates of the members as prime recruiting grounds. By the winter of 1966, the original membership quota of 600 had been filled, although serious obstacles had been encountered. Not all the large owners wanted to join, and out of thousands of share-croppers, only a few hundred could be included in the 600-member quota. The most common specific complaint heard during interviews and bar conversations was that the organizers had al-ready proved themselves corrupt in their first cooperative venture and that fifteen founding members were frauds and worse. Many waited to see if funds would mysteriously evaporate after the pro-ceeds of the first harvest had come in. Still others said they had gone it alone all their lives and were not about to change now, despite charges of egoism from the cooperativists. Nevertheless, there was enough confidence in the cooperative to create, during the 1967 campaign, a waiting list of an additional 600 cultivators asking for admission.

It is too soon to say what types of relationships will develop between sharecroppers and owners linked in the cooperative. However, several observations about the cooperative can be made that bear on its impact on landlord-tenant relationships in the dis-trict. First, although the cooperative presently includes only a minority of owners, it guarantees the commercial success of their holdings under the present sharecropping system while they learn how to implement mechanization. At the same time, it will slow the outmigration of *rabassaires*, which has been occurring at a rapid rate since the 1950s. This check on migration may, in turn, slow the spread of mechanization and also check the demise of the sharecropping system through attrition. Yet it does not prevent the owners from dislodging sharecroppers by payment of indemnities at a later date. Second, the state is now made responsible for providing the only effective solution to the revaluation of Alto Panadés table wines. This makes the owners economically depen-dent upon the state after they had already become its political dependents at the turn of the century. Economic initiative, a pre-rogative once fought for zealously by the Catalan bourgeoisie, has now become the government's uncontested area of strength. This is a change not hitherto experienced by any segment of the Catalan bourgeoisie.

This reversal has produced two major historical paradoxes in the

Alto Panadés. First, although the *rabassa morta* contract was adopted in part to prevent the development of a proletariat in agrarian Catalonia, today the state and the owners have joined to proletarianize the countryside at the expense of the *rabassaire*. This has been done not only by the introduction of mechanized viticulture in the district, but by the arrival of industry from Barcelona, which absorbs nearly all the *rabassaires* who have forsaken sharecropping. Second, the formation of a district cooperative dominated by the owners, but allowing membership to sharecroppers, shows the extent to which the large proprietors have changed under the Franco regime. Until recently, cooperativism was an institution of radical sharecroppers, forged in an atmosphere of hostility to the large proprietors, who saw in it the seeds of their economic destruction. Now cooperativism promises to be the economic salvation of these large proprietors and provides another link in the chain of their increasing dependency upon the state.

In the context of the agrarian transformation of the Alto Panadés, the *rabassaire* remains almost an anachronism, albeit a very visible one. Though the vast majority of vineyards are still cultivated by sharecroppers, there are unmistakable signs of the disintegration of this class. The most spectacular index of their condition is the decline in population of many sharecropper villages (Anon. 1966:8). This tendency toward population decline is most notable in the gentle slopeland that was once *rabassa morta* territory in its classic form.[19] In addition to the general decline of the viticulture economy, lack of transportation facilities keeps the sharecroppers of this zone from reaching the cooperative on the valley floor. Thus they cannot hope for relief.

A noticeable feature of the sharecropper population that remains on the land is age. The fields are tended by men over 45, dressed in baggy black corduroys covered with patches. All the young men have sought employment in the shops and factories, leaving their fathers in the fields as the remains of a past era. The fathers stay on in the fields in large part because it is difficult for them to get jobs in the factories, which prefer to hire younger men. Many also claim that factory work is akin to slavery and that they prefer the independence of the vineyards to industrial employment. These middle-aged *rabassaires* are not going down without a struggle, however dark their future appears. Faced with inadequate revenues from viticulture, many sharecroppers try to supplement their earnings by raising chickens in the courtyards of their houses and selling them on the open market. This economic alternative was made possible by the importation of American chicken feeds and chicken-raising techniques, which allow a large number of chickens to be raised in a small space. Prior to the importation of these techniques, sharecroppers simply kept a few chickens, which ran around loose in the courtyards. However, so many sharecroppers and large proprietors now raise fowls that chicken prices have plummeted steadily in the last few years. Earnings from chicken raising help the *rabassaire* eke out a living; they do not lead him to a new prosperity.

A further sign of the deteriorating position of the *rabassaire* is the disappearance, since 1960, of landlord-tenant lawsuits over land tenure.[20] The *rabassaire* can no longer view his sharecropping contract as a vehicle leading to acquisition of land in his own right. Nor do his sons show any interest in inheriting whatever small plots he may acquire. Given these conditions, the sharecropper simply does not bother to contest the inevitable. One of the closest links, albeit a negative one, between *rabassaire* and landlord – the lawsuit – has passed into history.

Perhaps the most obvious feature of the *rabassaire's* economic plight is the exodus from the villages of youth of sharecropper origins. Since 1960, light industry has burgeoned in the Alto Panadés, as a result of the *comarca's* proximity to Barcelona. Small new factories (producing cement, fertilizer, ceramics, animal feeds) are clustered along the main highway to Barcelona; more locate in the *comarca* each year. In addition to the factories, machine shops and construction trades are booming as the result of mechanization and the expansion of tourism into the district. Employment opportunities are so abundant that approximately 5,000 Castilian migrants have located in the Alto Panadés since 1950 (*Ponencia de Población* 1966:10). A strong attraction of industrial employment is the salary, which is three to four times the national minimum wage.[21] But perhaps the strongest attraction is that the salary is sufficient to permit a factory worker to participate in the growing consumer economy industry has brought in its train. A weekly pay check enables a worker to buy fashionable clothing, a radio, a motorcycle – tangible symbols of well-being in the Alto Panadés. It also allows him to consume daily aperitifs in the bars of Vilafranca, to gain entrance to a society that is faster paced than the somnolent life of a sharecropper village.

Participation in the industrial milieu and the consumer economy by the sons of *rabassaires* deals another blow to the moribund sharecropping system. In the past, all revenues earned by family members were pooled for the common familial good and administered by the tight-fisted head of the family. Drawing an independent salary, however, makes a son of a sharecropper potentially independent of his father (see Chapter 4). The consumer economy draws the young man's salary like a powerful magnet, and in so doing lays the ax to the father's historical position as family comptroller. But though the young man is less dependent on his father, he has also lost the relative autonomy of a *rabassaire*. As this process continues, side by side with the mechanization of the countryside, the institution of the *rabassa morta* contract, once the economic linchpin of the Alto Panadés, becomes an artifact of the past.

4

Erosion of the small property ethic: changing patterns of inheritance and marriage

Until 1960, family organization in the Alto Panadés (and elsewhere in Catalonia) was regulated by rules that simultaneously governed marriage and inheritance. These rules correspond to what Arensberg and Kimball refer to as a "marriage-succession system"[1] and have also been discussed in detail for Andorra by Stancliffe (1966). The principal juridical tenets of this system are the *hereu-pubilla* system of designating heirs and the *capitols matrimonials* system of regulating property transfer at the time of the heir's marriage.[2]

The "hereu-pubilla" marriage-inheritance system: fathers, heirs, and second sons

The *hereu-pubilla* inheritance system designates one child of a property holder as heir of his property. Formally, this child is the firstborn son of the property owner *(el hereu)*. If the property holder has no sons, the firstborn daughter *(la pubilla)* becomes the heir. At the time of the heir's marriage, the exact nature of the inheritance is stated in the document known as the marital charters *(capitols matrimonials)* drawn up by the two sets of parents of the betrothed. The Catalan marriage-inheritance system resembles the institution of primogeniture, but to consider it in this light only is to lose sight of the facts and spirit of the system. The *hereu-pubilla* inheritance system and the *capitols matrimonials* are two aspects of the larger structure of family organization in rural Catalonia. Historically, the aims of the Catalan property-holding families were not simply the maintenance of property, but the expansion of holdings and the scope of economic endeavor. The whole family organization was a strategy to achieve those ends. The Catalan family structure also had political overtones in a broad ideological sense;

because it was predicated on a strategy for the economic betterment of the family, it became a familial repository for the twin
Catalan ideals of property ownership and social mobility. Let us
analyze these major points in turn.

Actual family units in the Alto Panadés vary in composition, size,
and geographic dispersal of personnel. Despite this wide variation,
each property-holding family unit has a fixed structural maximum
of relatives in close contact with each other. This maximum unit I
refer to as the "family combine," because it is a group that combines its resources in a common strategy. In the Alto Panadés the
family combine is potentially composed of a property-owning adult
male, one set of grandparents, either father's or mother's brothers,
and all their children. Sometimes the group members all live in
one house together, but usually only some of these relatives do so.
The either/or categories of relationship refer to who (the man or the
woman) owns the house that is the base of the family combine. If it
is the house of the wife's family, then it is her brothers and parents
who occupy it; if it belongs to the husband's family, then his relatives live there. Whether all these people live together is irrelevant
to the organizational integrity of the combine. What is important is
how they fan out through society and what kind of contacts they
maintain with each other. Members of the combine may even live
in other villages or cities, but during the year, all visit the combine's base house *(casa pairal)*. To accommodate these visits, the
casa pairal, regardless of the social class of the owner, is frequently
far larger than it need be to accommodate the number of people
who live there permanently. No matter how grave their differences, members of the combine rarely permit information about
family endeavors to pass outside the portals of the *casa pairal*.[3]

The internal structure of the family combine can be discussed
best by starting with the role of the heir, who is the guarantor of
the stability of the combine. At the time of his marriage, he receives title to all productive property his father owns through the
capitols matrimonials. Whatever terms are written into this document are irrevocable before the law; the father cannot disinherit
his heir after the *capitols* are signed. But although he has title to
the productive property of his father, the *hereu* does not gain
direct control over this property. In over 99 percent of the *capitols*
I observed in the Vilafranca notary, the father retained rights of

disposition. By retaining the rights of disposition, the father guarantees that his son will not sell any portion of the inherited property until the father's death.

Instead of gaining full control of his father's property at the time of his marriage, the *hereu* enters a long period of apprenticeship in the management of his father's holdings. When the heir receives title to his father's property, the older man usually is still physically robust and able to continue making all key decisions concerning family enterprises. In fact, he is usually unwilling to allow the heir to take initiative in making such decisions, for fear the young man's inexperience might lead him to make decisions unfavorable to the interests of the combine. Thus the heir is subjected to a long period of handling small administrative details of the business, or is even consigned to physical labor on the family's lands. The long apprenticeship is designed to make the heir a conservative administrator of the family patrimony, rather than a speculative businessman. His role is not to increase the size of the family holdings, but merely to conserve whatever properties constitute his inheritance. The success or failure of the *hereu* is described in terms of administration: "He has known how to manage [his patrimony] well" (*"ha sabido administrar bien"*) and "He is a clumsy administrator" (*"es pésimo administrador"*) are two common descriptions applied to heirs.

The essentially conservative role of the *hereu* is quite different from the role of the second son (*caballer*). In contrast to the heir, the *caballer* must seek to diversify the family interests and/or holdings, which often involves a considerable amount of risk. In order for the *caballer* to do this, he must be launched by his family through direct capitalization, through family contacts, or both. His family subsidizes his training (if any is involved) or helps defray the cost of establishing him in his own business or uses its contacts to place him in some enterprise. In return for this aid, the *caballer* is expected to use his profession in the service of the family combine, if they have need of it. If the *caballer* fails (e.g., goes broke or is fired), the *hereu* must take him back into the *casa pairal* and help him recoup for another start.

The *caballer* has yet another stake in the patrimony, which he will collect on the death of his father. When the father dies, all his offspring receive an inheritance known as the "legitimate share" (*llegitim*). The *llegitim* is one-quarter of the total cash value of the father's holdings, divided equally among all his offspring, including the *hereu*. Thus, if the father has four children, each receives one-sixteenth of the monetary value of the patrimony. Although the *llegitim* is computed on the value of the paternal estate and property can be transferred as part of the inheritance, the *hereu* usually pays the other heirs the cash value of their share. He does this to avoid breaking up the property acquired by his ancestors. Thus, when the *capitols matrimonials* are drawn up, the cash value of the father's holdings is stipulated in the contract, in addition to the list of physical properties (houses, lands, businesses) constituting the estate. From this figure, shares of the *llegitim* are computed.

Social class and inheritance

Both the nature of the inheritance and the position of the *caballer* are functions of social class. Although the organizing principle of the family combine is the same for all property-owning classes, the productive and social resources available to each class differ widely, and the range of strategies possible differs for each class. Not only the business aspects of these strategies vary; matters of life style differ as well. While it is virtually impossible to provide precise statistical frequencies of the various strategies that are adopted by the different classes, it is possible to establish the range of strategies and styles available to each class.

The most spectacular inheritances and the widest range of life styles are, of course, those of the haute bourgeoisie. Minimally the *hereu* of such a family can expect to inherit upon his marriage (and control upon his father's death) a substantial agrarian holding (at least 20 hectares), control of at least one commercial establishment (frequently related to the land, e.g., a winery), a group of rental properties (real estate is the traditional backstop of all other forms of economy), and the *casa pairal* itself. It would be a paltry inheritance that did not equal 12 million pesetas (approximately $170,000), which is considered by local bank officials to be a fortune.

Such an inheritance is not typical of this class, but rather forms the bottom of the inheritance scale for a wealthy bourgeois family. More typical would be an inheritance in land of more than 100 hectares: thirty-six out of fifty heirs of wealthy families in my interview sample had inherited this much or more land. All owned at

Estate house (masia) of a large champagnery

least one commercial venture directly, over half (twenty-seven out of fifty) were outright owners of more than one, and over three-fourths (thirty-nine out of fifty) held shares in more than one company. Nearly all (forty-five out of fifty) had more than one rental property or at least shares or joint ownership in them. Typically, these properties were apartment buildings in Vilafranca, Barcelona, or along the coast. A continued housing shortage in these areas augurs well for investors in urban real estate. Curiously, none of the fifty individuals interviewed either owned or had shares in a seaside hotel, ·in spite of the tourist boom, although three held properties in Spanish middle-class summer home developments in the mountains (as opposed to the coast).

In a few instances, the inheritance was much larger and more complex than the typical inheritances just described. These special cases delineate the maximum inheritances in the Alto Panadés.[4] The largest inheritance I encountered involved two estates totaling some 350 hectares, two factories, a bank, three companies, a bar, five houses, three apartments, an indeterminate number of rental properties, and a seat on the Barcelona stock exchange. In another case, a champagnery with 10 miles of underground caves and its industrial plant had passed to single heirs for about 100 years. Yet another case involved the transmission of several estates with an aggregate of more than 1,000 hectares, accompanied by wine businesses of international scope, plus a large number of rental properties. While these cases are exceptional, they illustrate the magnitude of wealth some individuals have inherited.

Interview data suggest several important observations about this class that set it apart from other classes in the Alto Panadés. First, the wealthy bourgeoisie is the only class in the *comarca* that has property and economic activities outside the Alto Panadés. It is common, for example, for these people to have more than one estate, only one of which is in the Alto Panadés. The same is true of businesses and rental properties, many of which lie either in the province of Tarragona or in the city of Barcelona. Many also own homes in Barcelona and could not function without their web of commercial contacts in the Catalonian metropolis. Additionally, twelve out of the fifty interviewed directly participated in export-import businesses, some involving extensive foreign contacts. This is by no means a rural elite tied to the somnolent economy of a rural backwater. It participates directly in the economies of Catalonia as a whole, the Spanish nation, and foreign countries as well.

Second, just as their economic participation transcends the limits of the *comarca,* so do their social origins. Four families can trace their origins and properties back to the early 1500s (in each case, the family received land as a consequence of the Decree of Guadalupe); fifteen others owe their holdings in the Alto Panadés to a paternal investment in the area thirty or forty years ago when the family was based in either Barcelona or Tarragona. Most of the others in the sample gained holdings in the Alto Panadés during the nineteenth-century bourgeois colonization, entering the *co-marca* mainly from Barcelona and generally maintaining strong social and economic ties there. The dispersion of property and contacts distinguishes this class from all others in the *comarca*, just as their wealth operates to the same end.

A third striking aspect of the haute bourgeoisie concerns the lack of formal preparation of the *hereu* to administer such diverse property and so much wealth. In the case of agrarian properties, for example, only three heirs I interviewed had any technical preparation that would help them oversee their estates. Only ten had been to the university, where they studied matters totally unrelated to agriculture. Eight of these men took degrees in law; none practiced it, however. They had, as they said, *"profesiones sin ejercer"* ("professions they never exercised"). Only two others had even taken courses in commerce. The remainder had high school educations or less. The only apprenticeship heirs of this class traditionally served was to their own fathers. This tutelage, as one might expect in a system of rentier capitalism, was mainly concerned with matters of general commerce. Both the prospects and new requirements of agrarian modernization appear to be changing the upbringing of this generation's heirs (who do not yet have control over the properties they will inherit). Eight of these future heirs have received or were receiving technical training, either as agrarian engineer or agrarian surveyor, as are many of the *caballers* as well. As the realities of an owner's direct involvement in the cultivation of his land become more pronounced in the Alto Panadés, the number of heirs receiving more education of this sort will increase because these individuals are forced to assume more responsibility in the management of estates than their fathers had.

In the vast majority of cases, however, the *hereu* still has to administer many diverse types of family enterprises for which he has little preparation. Thus, he must depend on the services of right-hand men who have the technical capacity to do the essential work, frequently in his absence. Until very recently, this was generally the case in agriculture; less often in factories and commercial enterprises. Few proprietors knew much about agriculture; con-

sequently most of them depended upon the *masover* to oversee
their holdings. At present considerable effort has to be expended to
attract skilled agrarian labor, particularly workers with some
knowledge about how farm machinery is operated. Similar efforts
are made in the nonagrarian portions of family holdings. In short,
successful administration of the patrimony depends upon the heir's
ability to build up a core of loyal, technically competent retainers —
in anthropological language, a network of patron-client relationships. The noncontractual aspects of these relationships provide
the basis for the growing bar culture mentioned earlier (see Chapter 5 for further discussion).

Just as the quantity and quality of inheritances vary widely, so
are different strategies and life styles enjoyed by the heirs. Again,
only a description of the range of these strategies and styles can be
attempted here. One strategy is that of the classic rentier, exhibited clearly by twelve of the interviewees. Economically, this
involves minimum participation and concern with productive activities. In effect, the classic rentier does little except collect rents
from his property. Once the loyal core of dependents has been
acquired to manage the affairs of the rentier, he is free to dedicate
his life to more spiritually satisfying projects than productivity.
This personal elevation above material striving has engendered
what the local people consider some rather idiosyncratic and singu-
lar characters. One rentier devoted most of his adult years to collecting stamps and closely studying Homeric texts. Another was a
famous inventor, whose *casa pairal* became a laboratory, filled with
fantastic machines. Yet another spent most of his adult life trying
independently to invent a theory of evolution. Several were famed
principally for the parties they held with astonishing frequency on
their estates.

Apart from their individual pursuits, these classic rentiers seek
the company of their peers; most have traditionally enjoyed membership in at least one club where their peers congregate. Such
rentiers were the founders of the *Centro Agrícola* (see Chapter 5),
where they indulged themselves with games of dominos, while
slaking their thirst with horchata milk. Despite such life styles, the
classic rentiers of the Alto Panadés never achieved aristocratic
standing either within *comarcal* society or in Spain itself, much to
the regret of some of them. There are only four titles of nobility in

the *comarca*, all of them papal and dating only from the nineteenth century. Formal recognition of cultivated gentility is denied these rentiers, even if the substantive behavior is correctly acted out.

The classic rentier is the exception in the Alto Panadés and is in danger of becoming extinct as modernization renders his position each day more anachronistic. Much more common is an heir who takes some active interest in at least one of the productive enterprises he inherits. Twenty-seven of the heirs interviewed were active businessmen in their own right, involved in the management of at least one business, frequently two. Active participation in the purely agrarian parts of the family patrimony is rare among this group, at least at present. Most estates are not yet cultivated directly by their owners, and perhaps the heirs' preference for either industry or commerce can be explained by the fact that these young men have greater opportunities to exercise their talents in enterprises they can control thoroughly. An additional factor that probably lures them away from agriculture is the higher profit obtainable in the more speculative forms of enterprise such as real estate.

The life styles of these individuals reflect their economic orientation: They are public personalities, in constant touch seemingly with everyone in the Alto Panadés. As businessmen, they need contacts and spend much time courting them, in the bars and elsewhere. Though they consume a fair amount, they are in no way ostentatious about their consumerism. If they have a car, usually it is a small one; their clothing is generally the same as that of the popular classes, at least when they are on display. Their main arena of social action is the bar, although the more cultured among them belong to an association like the Museum of Vilafranca. Their life style has a peripatetic quality: They seem to surface in all places, under all scenarios, and at all hours.

Finally, eleven of the interviewees of the wealthy class were vigorously prosecuting all aspects of their domains, including agriculture. I believe these individuals most closely embody the ideals of Catalonia concerning vigor in enterprise coupled with a measure of austerity. These men, quite varied in their individual personalities, are all deeply involved in the productive aspects of their holdings. Their interest in agriculture prompts them to be generally innovative, willing to try new techniques or even new crops. If they have wineries associated with their estates, then the

production of wine is carried out with artisanlike dedication, with a
constant search for improvement in quality and individuality in
elaboration. Though profit making is hardly anathema to them, the
process of productivity itself has come to be an obsession with
them. They have a quiet pride and vigor in their work that would
have excited the fancies of the nineteenth-century English political
economists.[5]

These men do not lead the life of appearances and free-wheeling
sociability common to most people in the *comarca,* and particularly
to most members of their own class. They are not insensitive to the
necessities and nuances of the bar games, but they play them only
to the minimum extent necessary to achieve their goals; they do
not become absorbed in them. In fact, these men are distinguished
by the amount of freedom of action they seek, on both economic
and social levels. Though they frequent the bars and belong to the
clubs, they also have more private and family life than do most
other people in the Alto Panadés. They have managed to cultivate
both serenity and integrity, qualities one cannot fail to notice in
their presence.

The *caballers* of wealthy families are ideally staked to a career,
generally in commerce and/or professions related to enterprises
already held by the family. Among the sample I interviewed, the
two professions the *caballers* most commonly studied for were law
(18 out of 201)[6] and business (16); these were followed by engineer-
ing (8), agrarian surveying (6), medicine (4), and pharmacy (3).
Most *caballers* (134 out of 201) had no formal career preparation of
any kind.[7] Whatever professions they had come to exercise had
developed out of their fathers' contacts. As of 1969, formal education had much more to do with the status of an individual than with
the productive performance of a family; however, a trend toward
economic rationality in the training of *caballers* (and heirs as well)
seems to be discernible.

The careers of all the *caballers* of the wealthy class have one
thing in common: They increasingly require more education than
that provided by the public schools and consequently involve large
expenditures on the part of the parent that cannot be afforded by
the other social classes.[8] The *caballer's* father is expected personally to compensate for his son's lack of training or inadequate training by using his contacts to assure the boy's success. Thus the
father of a *caballer* who is a mediocre graduate of the University in

Barcelona is expected to provide his son with a host of contacts and a suitable office in the metropolis. This is referred to as "backing." In contrast, the son of a petit bourgeois who struggled through law school could be expected to wind up with a poorly furnished office and a very short list of clients that it would take him years to increase.

If the opportunity presents itself, the *caballer* is expected to purchase property in his own right. The vast majority of the *caballers* in my sample had invested in rental properties rather than in productive enterprises. At present, nearly all *caballers* concentrate on their professions, rather than attempting to acquire property or devoting much time to working with property they own. This concentration on professional activities, as we shall see, appears to be a recent phenomenon in the Alto Panadés. Until a generation ago, property acquisition was much easier than it is at present, and much more emphasis could be placed upon it than is now feasible.

Perhaps the most critical role of the *caballer* in relation to the family combine are those of counselor and information broker. Ideally, the profession of the *caballer* complements the major businesses of the *hereu*. Thus, if the family needs technical advice that the *caballer's* profession enables him to supply, he is called on to provide such advice. Each *caballer* also furnishes information he gains from his own set of contacts to the wider family information pool. This information usually concerns commercial trends and opportunities and their bearing on familial holdings. Information pooling usually takes place during the *caballer's* frequent visits to the *casa pairal*.

The inheritance patterns of the other social classes in the *comarca* are much less complicated than those of the haute bourgeoisie. Yet the operations of the *hereu-pubilla* system in these classes are important because they give social coherence in the form of a dense web of kinship relations that transcend class lines. Within almost any local family, one can find *rabassaires*, petits bourgeois, and working-class individuals, frequently all in a single (or at most two) generations. Both the reduced level of property and the restricted scope of their economic activities lead inexorably to the fanning out of family personnel into the popular classes, generation after generation. Hence these classes have interlocking origins and destinies.

The heirs of petit bourgeois families have tiny inheritances compared with those of the haute bourgeoisie. Furthermore, these inheritances are located within the *comarca;* the popular classes of the Catalonian cultural tradition are nothing if not local. A typical inheritance of this class includes a small business, frequently a one-room store but on occasion something as substantial as a small hotel; a vineyard not exceeding 10 hectares, and usually between 1 and 3 hectares in size; and a small rental property. These diverse properties, if worked diligently, provide a comfortable although by no means luxurious existence for the heir and his family. There are no leisurely rentiers in this class, but rather a great number of energetic and conscientious small businessmen.

The genesis of these businesses is one of the most absorbing chapters in regional history. Nearly all of the 200-odd small stores and other businesses in rural villages and in Vilafranca as well originated from sharecropper investments by *caballers.* Characteristically, the father of a *rabassaire* second son would scrimp and save to purchase a business or a share of one for his *caballer.* The *caballer,* frequently starting with a small store no larger than a single room, would spend long hours, year after year to nourish his small business, ultimately becoming moderately prosperous. If the business is a grocery store (as many are), the *caballer* can sometimes also count on his father to furnish some foods seasonally at greatly reduced costs. He is, in turn, able to offer small rebates to his relatives who patronize his store. Such a store is a source of great familial pride; it validates the regional belief that the inheritance system is a principal reason for the greater prosperity and social mobility of Catalonians compared with other Spaniards.

Although the *hereu-pubilla* system has led to the creation of many small businesses in the *comarca,* most *caballers* do not at present enjoy such good fortune. Even second sons of families who have already reached petit bourgeois standing are unlikely to acquire their own businesses. Only a handful are sent to the university to learn a profession; most are lucky to have a year's enrollment in a commercial course after completing high school at age fourteen. Most second sons usually seek clerical, white-collar jobs in large firms in the area or in Barcelona. Thus the same system that provides for the evolution of small business in the *comarca* also creates a profusion of upper-echelon proletarians.

If the position of heirs and second sons among the petite bourgeoisie is delicate, the position of these individuals among the

Masover family

rabassaires is precarious. The heir of a sharecropper receives whatever little piece of property his father accumulated, his house, and his tools. The *hereu* can look forward to receiving his father's contractual obligations with the owner of the land for whom his father was a *rabassaire* if the traditional contractual arrangements are in force on the owner's property. As these arrangements are becoming less common each year and the economic position of the sharecroppers is declining, more and more heirs are simply renouncing their inheritance and joining the ranks of the proletariat.

Rarely, the second son of a *rabassaire* is staked to a small business; most seek jobs as skilled workmen, which pay well by local standards and project these youths into the consumer economy and its attendant joys. The most common trades for these youths seem to be construction work and hotel work, in about equal proportion. Many find employment in factories. Very few stay on the land in any capacity; those who do, work for wages, not as sharecroppers. It is interesting to note that these new jobs have been created by the very process of modernization that has pushed most *rabassaires* out of agriculture.

Sharecropper hamlet

It should be emphasized that the *hereu-pubilla* system of marriage and inheritance can operate only among the propertied classes and does not apply to all people of the Catalonian cultural tradition living in the Alto Panadés. Working-class families cannot practice this form of inheritance because they lack property. Upon the death of a working-class father, his belongings and cash pass to his widow. If she is deceased, these belongings are divided equally among all their chidlren, male and female alike.

From an economic standpoint, the *hereu-pubilla* inheritance system seems to operate best in an economy that is modern, yet small in scale – where the actual properties are small, numerous, and somewhat commercially fluid over time. Hence the system seems to be predicated upon the acquisition of property (or at least, as in the past, long-term tenure arrangements) and, its long-term maintenance by the single heir. If this is true, it seems unlikely that this system can endure much longer because property is becoming more and more concentrated as businesses grow larger and more elaborate. This trend has all but eliminated the sharecroppers from this system, and a potential concentration of small businesses may soon threaten the petite bourgeoisie.

The larger kin group

The larger kin group is created by marriages. During the heyday of the *hereu-pubilla* inheritance system, marriages within the property-owning classes were arranged by heads of households, not by the individuals who were to be married. Marriage was strictly a business proposition that involved both a transfer of property and a potential business alliance between the heads of households. Transfer of property occurred in the form of a dowry, which was also written into the *capitols matrimonials*. The dowry consisted of money and/or household equipment for the bride-to-be (kitchenware, bedding, and clothing). If the bride-to-be was a *pubilla*, then part of her dowry consisted of the property of her father, to which she received full rights upon his death. Elegance of the dowry varied widely with social class. A *pubilla* of the wealthy bourgeoisie might bring with her into marriage a host of diversified properties. In contrast, one of the *capitols* I read concerning a marriage within the sharecropper class stipulated that the bride would bring only sheets, towels, a dozen pairs of underpants, a steamer trunk, and twenty dresses.

Business partnerships sometimes take place between the heads of intermarrying households. Among large landowners, these associations have led to cooperative buying of machinery and subsequent sharing of this machinery among members of the two households. In one instance, heads of four households united by marriage formed a viticulture cooperative for large landowners. The relatives formed the board of directors of this cooperative during its several years of existence. In other instances, new businesses were jointly capitalized by members of households allied by marriage.[9]

Business partnerships do not always follow marriage alliances, but business partnerships between affinal kin are always a good possibility. Unless a business partnership is actually consummated between the two houses, the larger kin group has very little cohesion. For this reason, people in the Alto Panadés frequently have difficulty explaining degrees of relationship to their official kin if they are not actively involved with them in some endeavor. Among the wealthy bourgeoisie, the rate of intermarriage has been so high for the past four generations that many members of this class can point to any *casa pairal* and state that they have relatives there. Yet frequently they cannot remember the relatives' first names or exactly how they are related. The best explanation they can furnish is, "We are all related." These relationships, no longer vital and not remembered in detail, were important perhaps two generations ago when a business partnership evolved out of a strategic marriage. In brief, fortunes of particular combines vary from generation to generation, and so do the opportunities for strategic marriages. According to the economic strength of intermarrying households at a given moment, alliances between members of the larger kin group are taut or lax.

If we consider the *hereu-pubilla* marriage-inheritance system as a strategy (or a series of strategies) for the accumulation of property and its transmission, we gain some insights into another dimension of Catalan regionalism. As we have seen earlier, regional ideology emphasized the growing material prosperity of Catalonia, especially in comparison with other regions in Spain. This prosperity was not only the collective business of all Catalans, but was also related to the material prosperity of individuals. The prospect of social mobility is implicit, for example, in the *rabassa morta* contract.

Lest we conjure up a Catalan counterpart to the myth of Yankee individualism, it must be made clear that the *style* of social mobility was seen quite differently in Catalonia than in the United States in the early 1900s. Rather than focusing on the individual, unassisted and surmounting all obstacles to success with his monumental will, the Catalan image of social mobility was a protracted *familial* struggle to acquire property. Whereas the Yankee struggled as a manual laborer to acquire some property, the Catalan believed that one *worked* only if he had some *property* to work. A Catalan comparison between themselves, considered as a people, and other peoples living in the Iberian peninsula, goes as follows: "The Castilians go through life without working, without striking a blow, always looking for a sinecure. We in Catalonia have property; therefore, we work."[10]

Regional ideology viewed social mobility as the acquisition of property and its subsequent maintenance and expansion through the *hereu-pubilla* system (Maspons i Anglasells 1935:81). As I have mentioned earlier, this ideology was referred to as *pairalisme* (allegiance to the paternal house). The simplest manifestation of *pairalisme* was a perfect acting out of the marriage-inheritance system; one branch of the family maintained rural property and seeded other branches (through the *caballers*) in the metropolitan business world. Thus, from a small rural estate, a great estate grew and captains of industry were simultaneously established (Maspons i Anglasells 1935:81–3).

There was a good deal of truth in the claim that the marriage-inheritance system would lead to social mobility. Although few *rabassaires* ever became part of the haute bourgeoisie, many did acquire properties; many of the small businesses in the villages and in Vilafranca were established through the *hereu-pubilla* system; and many of the haute bourgeoisie used it to enhance their already considerable wealth. Given the fact that the system often worked, it is hardly surprising that it appeared as part of the political ideology of Catalan regionalism, as a vigorous and beneficial regional custom that set Catalonia apart from other regions of Spain. However, like all other Catalan institutions that contributed to the regionalist spirit, the marriage-inheritance system was marked by ambiguities and contradictions. A mechanism for familial advancement, it was at the same time often the source of intrafamilial discord and tension. For the system to work, some persons, notably the heir, were constrained economically and emotionally so that others might prosper. At present, economic changes in the Alto Panadés are bringing out the sources of conflicts within the family with increasing frequency and threaten to bury the marriage-inheritance system altogether.

Conflict and change in the "hereu-pubilla" system

Two conflicts exist in family combines organized around the *hereu-pubilla* inheritance system; both concern the position of the *hereu*. The first conflict is between the heir and his father, and concerns the long apprenticeship the heir serves before acquiring full rights to the patrimony. Because of the sensitive position the heir will hold as guarantor of his siblings' prosperity, his father sometimes demands from him extraordinary demonstrations of family loyalty. The father fears that the *hereu* may collect all the patrimony on his death and not aid his siblings, or that he may be injudicious in money matters and be forced to sell some or all of the patrimony. The *hereu* who behaves this way is known as a "stray bullet," and there are many stories about such heirs.[11]

If such fears possess the heir's father, he may become a tyrant who makes life unbearable for his son. This is particularly true in wealthy bourgeois families, where much property is at stake. While the *caballers* are already established in their professions, and enjoying relative wealth and independence, the situation of the heir is quite the reverse. He may well be working at his father's office at prewar wages, and he must do this unflinchingly to demonstrate that he is loyal to the family. In several cases among the wealthy bourgeoisie I interviewed, the fathers had furnished very modest apartments for the heirs and provided the minimum accoutrements appropriate to the class – a small car, a television set, etc. The heir himself could afford none of these things on his small salary, although his brothers' salaries allowed them to live in much fancier places and take long summer vacations.

The heir's period of deprivation may last into very late manhood, depending on the longevity of his father. "I only have ten years of life left that I could enjoy, and that guy [his father] is still as strong as an oak," said one middle-aged heir to me. In these cases, when the father becomes a tyrant, the heir sullenly waits many years for the old man to die. Although I do not know the statistical frequency of this phenomenon, it is common enough to have a name – "the heir's curse." Many such relationships are visible in all the property-owning classes. The structure of the relationship is potentially conflict-laden because the father must always check the egocentric tendencies of the heir to do as he pleases with the patrimony.

The *hereu* does not have to accept paternal tyranny. He has the option of abdicating as heir in favor of another sibling. That is, he can choose between enjoying the relative independence of a profession or trade and waiting to receive the patrimony. Often the heir does abdicate, although abdication becomes less common as the wealth involved in the inheritance increases. If the heir abdicates, the father simply designates a younger son as heir. The presence of *caballers* who have become *hereus* through the abdication of the firstborn son suggests that the *hereu-pubilla* system is not strictly one of primogeniture. What is important is not that the firstborn son (or daughter) inherits, but that one offspring is in the position of conserving the property base of the family.

A second common conflict, often related to the first, involves the relationships between the *hereu* and his brothers and sisters. This conflict takes place when the father dies and the *hereu* must distribute the shares of the *llegitim* to his siblings. As noted earlier, the *llegitim* is stipulated in the *capitols matrimonials*, and what each heir will receive is written into this legal document. However, the *llegitim* is calculated on the basis of what the father *claims* his holdings are worth in cash. Because there is a state tax on inheritance, the father usually declares the value of the estate to be much less than it actually is; he assumes that all heirs will agree among themselves about the actual value of the estate and will receive their shares accordingly. In practice, however, the *hereu* may decide not to honor this tacit agreement. At the time of his father's death, he may attempt to pay his brothers and sisters the exact amount stated in the *capitols matrimonials*, and his siblings may retaliate by suing him. When the petition is brought to court, the judge sends an assayer to evaluate the estate. Based on the findings of the assayer, the judge allots reassessed shares to all litigants.

This conflict is not necessarily a function of economics alone, for in many cases the amounts contested for are small and the price of litigation is always high. "Better a bad agreement than a favorable legal settlement," is a stock phrase used to describe the hazards of entering into a lawsuit. Lawsuits involving less than a total value of 20,000 pesetas ($285 by 1972 currency values) are so common that a special section of the court is required to deal with them.[12] Yet $285 is much less than the average annual earnings of a sharecropper in the Alto Panadés, and legal proceedings greatly reduce the amount actually received, frequently by as much as half. If the litigation proves unprofitable for the *caballers*, it is equally unprofitable and unpleasant for the *hereu*, who not only has to pay more to his relatives and lawyers but must also pay higher land taxes to the state over a period of years. Why these lawsuits, with marginal benefits and potential losses for one or both sides, are so common cannot be explained in economic terms alone.

An *hereu* must make some calculations about the economic feasibility of denying his siblings their share of the patrimonial wealth. He may calculate that the cost of litigation will deter the other heirs from taking him to court. Or he may believe that his contacts in the legal profession (including the judge) are strong enough to get the case thrown out of court. Though these alternatives have doubtless been applied by many an heir, both the high cost of lawsuits and the familial ethic inhibit basing such a maneuver on solely economic considerations. The psychological position of the *hereu* in relation to his father and his siblings plays a part as well. Frequently the long apprenticeship of the heir is fraught with personal bitterness and frustration against his father and his siblings. The *hereu* may view his father as a tyrant and his brothers and sisters as burdens upon his own livelihood. While his siblings are enjoying relative freedom, he is constrained by the dictates of his father, who is a judge of all his actions. Should the father come to think ill of him, he may be disinherited at the time of his marriage. Furthermore, if it is obvious to all that he is plagued by a tyrannical father and/or parasitic siblings, he may also become an object of public ridicule for accepting the situation.

Under such pressures and insecurities, an heir can easily come to harbor deep-seated grudges against his father and his siblings. Because collection of his inheritance depends on his remaining in his father's good graces, the sisters and brothers become the targets of his revenge, once the old man is dead and buried. The juridical vehicle of his revenge is the *llegitim*, which he uses to bring his siblings into conflict with him. Though in some cases the *llegitim* involves an important amount of money and supplies an economic motive for the heir's action against his siblings, financial gain is not usually the real issue. Dragging an inheritance case into court is best explained as a public demonstration by the heir that he is renouncing the whole family combine. The *hereu*, through the court case, is announcing to his siblings and to the world, that they can go their own way without further assistance from him.

Until recently, conflicts between family members over matters of inheritance seldom reached the lawsuit stage. But all the lawyers I consulted reported an enormous increase of such cases within the past ten years, the majority of which were small claims. After hearing many accounts of the intensity with which these suits were fought, I began to wonder if the marriage-inheritance system was disintegrating. My suspicions were heightened by continued reports of the decline of arranged marriages. I had previously been skeptical of these reports because I had been able to document large numbers of people who were involved in the marriage-inheritance system, both as heirs and as partners in arranged marriages, and I assumed that nearly everyone with any kind of property adhered to this system. Those who said they married for love or claimed they would abdicate as heirs if their fathers so much as said a cross word to them were, I suspected, lying to me to conceal the true details of their family relationships. But my researches in the parish office and the office of the notary public uncovered information that suggested that people I had taken for liars were actually telling the truth. In the parish office, where I had been checking various details of marriages made in Vilafranca over several decades, I noted that the marriage cohort for an average year since the civil war had been slightly over 200 people (100 couples).[13] In the notary's office, where *capitols matrimonials* are made between families, I found statistical information on the yearly frequency of *capitols* since 1941.[14] From 1941 to 1960, *capitols* were made, on the average, thirty-seven times per year.[15] However, since 1960, no more than eight have been made in any year, and only one was made in all of 1966. I was therefore obliged to revise my original impression and begin to consider why the marriage-inheritance system appeared to be in its death throes.

Decline of the system

The sharp decline in the numbers of *capitols matrimonials* since 1960 can most readily be explained by the kind of modernization that is taking place in the *comarca*. Property is simultaneously becoming more concentrated and more expensive. Because this marriage-inheritance system is predicated on the acquisition of property, it is doomed to precipitous extinction (the decline is marked in only a decade) after at least 800 years of existence. The economics of the demise of the institution are rather obvious; the social ramifications of this change are not. Some of them lie in the realm of speculation, as they are not yet resolved; others touch the ideological component of regionalism profoundly and simultaneously affect the loves and lives of Catalonians not yet grown up. The following brief synthesis of the present situation highlights the salient features of these changes.

The basic economics of the change involve the spillover of industry from Barcelona, the growth of local industry, the increase of the tourist trade on the nearby coast, and the rapid and profound penetration of consumerism into the Alto Panadés. The first three factors are steadily causing the value of land to rise in the *comarca*, forcing all landowners to think of their properties in terms of real estate rather than as a steady source of wealth from agriculture.

Land-hungry industrial concerns and, to a lesser extent, real estate speculators offer four and five times the agricultural value of a piece of land, particularly of land readily accessible to the Barcelona-Valencia highway. The impact of this penetration in the *comarca* is reflected in a variety of ways. On the valley floor along the highway, factories (many of them foreign enterprises) have already replaced prime vineyard. Along the mountainous rim of the valley, sharecroppers and small holders have been leaving marginal vineyards, and vacation houses for the metropolitan middle class are springing up in their place. Even the haute bourgeoisie landholders have stopped trying to purchase more land for agriculture, claiming they simply cannot afford it. Instead of their characteristic expansionism, these agriculturalists are now concerned mainly to get their sharecroppers off the land they already own, in the hopes of increasing their profit margins.

The expansion of the economy in other areas than agriculture, which remains stagnant, puts premium pressure on small holders to sell out at a good price and search for more remunerative employment elsewhere. Two decades ago, a sharecropper who owned 1 or 2 hectares of vineyard could view this property as a modest but crucial source of income. Now, low prices for wine have made earnings from these plots trivial. The sons of these sharecroppers view this income as insignificant compared with what they can earn as wage workers in construction or in factories and are increasingly disposed to part with the family land.

Consumerism also plays a role in the dissolution of the marriage-inheritance system. Money that once was used to acquire property now goes increasingly to accumulate the consumer goods that are readily available in the *comarca*. A man's well-being is often gauged by the clothing he can purchase, whether he can afford a motorcycle or even a car, and whether he is able repeatedly to stake his friends to drinks and snacks in the local bars. The tangible symbols of success, the imagery of social mobility, relate increasingly to the consumer economy. Success, once measured in terms of ability to accumulate productive property, is now increasingly measured in terms of nonproductive tokens (consumer goods).

Viewed from this perspective, conflict over the *llegitim* becomes intelligible in another way besides mere psychological frustration of the heir. The presence of the consumer economy puts pressure on individuals to spend whatever capital they have, rather than to pool it in a common familial effort to acquire property. The heir is as much subject to this pressure (perhaps more so, if he has endured years of privation prior to receiving his inheritance) as are his siblings. The court fight over the *llegitim* represents a formal dissolution of the heir's obligations to his siblings under the marriage-inheritance system. Once freed of these obligations, the heir can spend on consumer goods money he would once have had to hold in reserve to back the ventures of his siblings.

In sum, the marriage-inheritance system is being dissolved by the economic transformation of the Alto Panadés. Although partitive inheritance is fast becoming the rule for persons of all social classes, it cannot be said simply that one type of inheritance system is being replaced by another. The implications of the demise of the *hereu-pubilla* system are far more profound to the people living in the Alto Panadés. The marriage-inheritance system structured the material aspirations of the generations that grew up when the institution was in full vigor and formally delineated the roles of parents and children toward each other. Inheritance is becoming unimportant to the life outlooks of the generation presently growing up in the Alto Panadés. The demise of the system also represents a further weakening of the regionalist ethic predicated in large part on the florescence of Catalan cultural institutions.

5

Public social organization: cultural associations and bar culture

The waning of the *rabassa morta* land-tenure system and the *hereu-pubilla* inheritance system is directly linked to the different economic opportunities brought about by the modernization of the *comarcal* economy by Franco's authoritarian regime. Nowhere are the political changes brought by modernization clearer, however, than in public social organization. Although economic opportunities abound for all classes in the Alto Panadés, these opportunities are no longer solely controlled by the Catalan bourgeoisie, but increasingly by the national government. The government allows neither class nor regional political organizations to usurp its economic control or to threaten its political preeminence. Thus, the main contrast between pre- and post-Franco public social organization is that prior to 1939 every adult male in the *comarca* had an explicit political orientation and education, along class or regional lines, or both. Opportunity for the expression of such political orientations was provided by the cultural associations that flourished following the 1850s, often with a dynamism independent of the bourgeois impulse that created them. A few of these associations continue to exist today, but under strict state controls. They have since 1960 been replaced as the most dynamic centers of public social organization by modern bars, where members of the bourgeoisie, technicians, and skilled workers compete for services, favors, and advancements in an explicitly apolitical context.

To facilitate the exposition of the transition between these two phases of public social organization, I have divided this chapter into two sections. The first describes the cultural associations of the *comarca* and the idioms attached to them; the second contrasts these with the coalition formation and idioms of bar culture in Vilafranca del Panadés.

Cultural associations

Chapters 2 and 3 described briefly the process by which the Catalan bourgeoisie colonized the countryside to protect and stabilize industrial holdings threatened by the vagaries of the Spanish economy. After the last Carlist war (1872–6) the needs of this class were two: on the local level, labor for the vineyards; on the national level, regional cohesion against the government in Madrid. The need for labor was temporarily solved by revival of the *rabassa morta* contract. To build regional cohesion against the Madrid government cultural associations were created to celebrate Catalanism and to create a sense of nationhood, which at the turn of the century could be expressed at the polls, under the vigilant eyes of the local *caciques*. Thus, the bourgeoisie subsidized these institutions financially, and while doing so promoted a regionalist folk culture designed to weld all classes of Catalans into a populist front against the central government.

I shall describe four cultural associations in the Alto Panadés: the *Casino de la Unión*, the *Centro Agrícola*, the *Sociedad la Principal*, and the *Ateneu Obrer*. All emerged in Vilafranca del Panadés. Though many voluntary associations throughout the *comarca* promoted Catalan regionalism (Mas i Perera 1932:155–81; Sabaté i Mill 1966), these four enjoyed far more popular participation than the others. Outlining the basic structure of these four associations and tracing their historical growth will explain most of the paradoxes inherent in the associational milieu.

The history of the *Casino de la Unión*, the first of the cultural associations in Vilafranca, exemplifies the path followed at a later date by other more overtly political groups. The *casino* was founded in 1853 by two prominent businessmen from Vilafranca. They launched their association with a lengthy statute proclaiming that "the object of this society is to provide individuals with honest past-times for which it will have salons of recreation, of reading and of legitimate gaming" (Sabaté i Mill 1966:3). The founding of an association dedicated to such aims may appear so prosaic as to merit no more than a passing comment, but in the Alto Panadés of the mid-1800s it proved an almost revolutionary event. Throughout the nineteenth century, colonization of the *comarca* had led to an enormous increase in population and economic prosperity; yet there were virtually no centers for secular entertainment. Prior to 1853 the only voluntary associations in the entire *comarca* were two Catholic brotherhoods. Sabaté i Mill (1966:4) describes one as being for wage-earning agriculturalists and the other for bourgeois conservatives; this contrasts sharply with the unity of classes aimed for by some of the associations after 1853. The only *public* establishments were a few taverns and billiard halls, which were shut after eight o'clock in the winter and nine o'clock in the summer (Sabaté i Mill 1966:5).

The *casino* became almost overnight a stopping place for everyone in the *comarca* and over the next thirty-three years grew steadily in membership and importance in the area. Particularly attractive to the local elite, the *casino* welcomed members of all classes in the Alto Panadés to the gaming tables and the weekly dances held on Saturday night (Mas i Perera 1932:198). Every day the *casino* was filled with groups of people clustered around indoor and outdoor tables drinking coffee, discussing the news, and playing cards. Many of the discussions concerned politics, especially the politics of regional prosperity, which were not yet of a Catalan nationalist hue. Brooding over the ardent café politicians of Vilafranca was the sepia likeness of General Prim[1] painted on the façade of the building. Inside the building were other portraits of General Prim, showing scenes from his more glorious military exploits (Sabaté i Mill 1966:5). Prim, a highly political man, was widely admired by bourgeois elements throughout Catalonia for his staunch advocacy of a federalist national government that would allow regional autonomy for Catalonia. Prim was also a close friend of Antony Fontanals, one of the founders of the *casino*.

The *casino*, however, was short-lived. Its formal termination anticipated the histories of later cultural associations in the Alto Panadés. In 1888 it was forced to close because one of the members of its directorate had placed illegal gambling tables in the *casino* and was using them to bilk the membership. Membership declined until all property of the society had to be sold at public auction to cancel the debts of the directorate (Sabaté i Mill 1966:8). The incident that forced the dissolution of the *casino* was not, however, the real cause of the decline in its popularity. The actual cause was the *rabassaire* question, which divided the membership politically. Elements of the petite bourgeoisie flocked to the voting lists of the Radical party, which advocated curbs on the growing economic and political power of the Catalan bourgeoisie and championed popular republicanism (Brenan 1962:298).[2]

The success of the Radical party and the prevalence of the petit bourgeois view on the *rabassaire* question led the rentiers to resent many of their fellow *casino* members. The rentiers left the *casino* as a body in 1879, the year the monarchy was restored. To celebrate the restoration of the monarchy and the temporary suspension of political parties, the rentiers created their own association, the *Centro Agrícola*, along what they imagined to be aristocratic lines. Though the membership of the new association was considered effete by local standards, the directorate consisted of large proprietors affiliated with diverse political interests within the Restoration government rather than with the industrial Catalan bourgeoisie. Included among the members of the *centro* were holders of papal titles and representatives of that section of the wealthy class of Catalans which favored the Restoration – principally simple rentiers with no metropolitan interests (Mas i Perera 1932:170; Sabaté i Mill 1966:7).

In 1906, the most popular of all the cultural associations in the Alto Panadés was founded. Known as the *Sociedad la Principal*, it was established by prosperous small businessmen from Vilafranca. This association was conceived of by its founders as genuine expression of Catalan regionalism. Members of all social classes were welcomed into the *sociedad*, which was organized around a variety of popular recreational activities, such as football, photography, *sardana* dancing, basketball, music, drama, and stamp collecting (Mas i Perera 1932:170).

Though the founders of the *sociedad* were drawn mainly from the Vilafranca petite bourgeoisie, its membership included large numbers of workers and *rabassaires*. Within the association, all formal political tendencies were represented: The *sociedad* served as the local political office for the traditional Catalan Left, but anarchists, socialists, and monarchists were prominent as well. Despite the political differences of the members, the political idiom of all contenders for offices within the association was Catalan and regionalist (Mas i Perera 1932:172). A focal point for all manner of recreational activities and political tendencies, the *sociedad* had by 1928 a membership of 7,000 people from all over the *comarca* (Mas i Perera 1932:173).

A fourth cultural association, the *Ateneu Obrer* (Workingman's Atheneum), thrived in the same era as the *Sociedad la Principal*. Founded in 1904, the *ateneu* was hypothetically dedicated to fomenting the class struggle against all segments of the Catalan bourgeoisie (Mas i Perera 1932:178). In addition to furnishing the

A xiquet in formation

usual bar and newspaper, it served as headquarters for radical politicians such as anarchist Salvador Segui, bent on organizing the working classes in Catalonia. But despite its ideological dedication to the class struggle, the *ateneu* was established and dominated by elements of the local petite bourgeoisie. The guiding spirit, P. Clavé, was a Catalan nationalist from Vilafranca, considered by local people of all social classes as one of the "fathers of the country."[3] Clavé was the son of a local carpenter and a firm believer in the social betterment of the working classes through the acquisition of culture. He believed anarchism to be the true expression of the workers' sentiments and therefore their legitimate political vehicle, but was himself emotionally committed to Catalan nationalism. His personal ambivalence was reflected in the format of the *ateneu:* Amid the bookracks cluttered with anarchist propaganda, the workers staged popular Catalan drama and amused themselves by performing Bach cantatas under the direction of Clavé (Mas i Perera 1932:180).

There is much confusion about the nature of the membership of the *ateneu.* Many people contend that it was principally composed of *rabassaires;* others say it was made up of workers from Vilafranca. Both analyses are true; though the base membership of the *ateneu* was indeed workers who lived in Vilafranca, most of them belonged in fact to sharecropper families who lived in the Alto Panadés.[4] As explained in Chapter 4, family loyalties often transcended economic loyalties based on social class in the *comarca.* It is precisely because the workers of Vilafranca were of sharecropper origin that they saw no contradiction between workingman's anarchism and Catalan nationalism. A contrast between workers' anarchism in Vilafranca, and workers' anarchism in Barcelona is illustrative in this context. The Barcelona *Confederación Nacional de Trabajo* (CNT) was pitted against the bourgeoisie (and violently so) throughout the twentieth century. The Barcelona anarchists were all of Castilian origin; those of Vilafranca were all Catalan and therefore ambivalent in their political thinking (Brenan 1962:202).

Because of its ideological emphasis, the *ateneu* did not attract as large a membership as the *casino* or the *Sociedad la Principal.* However, it is important because from its membership came three of the most dynamic officials of the municipal government during the Republic of 1931–6. Politically they represented the CNT, but they were able to work with Catalan nationalists drawn from the governing board of the *Sociedad la Principal* to bring about many municipal reforms that are still noticeable.[5] The *ateneu* was shut down in 1939, the first victim of the Franco regime's repression of Catalan and left-wing cultural associations.

Common themes run through the histories of all the associations in the Alto Panadés. First and foremost is the theme of Catalan nationalism, which appeared in all associations, regardless of the political sympathies of the membership. Anarchists and monarchists, workers and petite bourgeoisie all found a political rallying point in the ideology of Catalan nationalism. Irrespective of the class struggle, party politics, and personal inclinations, everyone was in some degree a Catalan nationalist, including the rentiers of the *Centro Agrícola*, who were among the first of that Catalan bourgeoisie to place class politics above regional politics. The associations appealed to Catalan nationalism. They monopolized the recreational life of an entire *comarca*. Members came to enjoy the dramas, the dances, the drinking, and the talking quite apart from the political ambience. And it so happened that the very language of recreation was that of Catalan regionalism: to dance a *sardana* instead of a waltz affirmed one's love of his homeland. In the same way, to appreciate the essence of *renaixença* drama, one had to be a Catalan. Thus the recreations of an average person, irrespective of his social class, were wrapped in the symbols of Catalan nationalism. Far from being the exclusive product of local or national political problems, the associations thrived because of their cultural and sentimental appeal to people in all walks of life (Mas i Perera 1932:185).

Another influence on the character of all the local associations was the political drive of the local bourgeoisie. The most dynamic agents in the transformation of the rural economy, these men were also the movers of local political life. Workers do not learn to like Bach cantatas and appreciate Wanda Landowska without coaching.[6] Like all social classes, the bourgeoisie was divided among several different political points of view, as we have seen. But one thing dominated the thinking of all the bourgeoisie, regardless of ideological position: the need to form alliances. All segments of the bourgeoisie, at one time or another, indulged in populist politics. They attempted to rally the political support of all classes of the Catalan cultural tradition. While the resultant coalitions were often unstable, Catalan nationalism provided a social bridge across class differences.

The bourgeois domination of the cultural associations was manifested not only in the advocacy of culture, but also in pragmatic efforts to better the economic lot of the members. All the associations in Vilafranca initiated medical, educational, and insurance plans for their members. Membership dues were applied to pay the expenses of these programs (Sabaté i Mill 1966:7). Emphasis in these programs was on the benefits people could receive by work-ing collectively rather than as individuals. By saving his money and putting it into associational dues, any man could better his life circumstances (Mas i Perera 1932:176). In addition, men went to the associations in search of other men who could help them solve their daily problems. Even though the associations were domi-nated by one social class, members of all social classes were rep-resented in all the associations. For example, a *rabassaire* could use the *Sociedad la Principal* to strike up a friendship with a large landowner; a factory owner could support the *Ateneu Obrer* in the hopes of personally satisfying workers' grievances. The associations provided a context in which men could meet and discuss anything over coffee and brandy or over a card table, and consequently consider each other in roles other than those of worker, factory owner, *rabassaire*, or rentier.

The four most prominent associations in Vilafranca were indeed related to the activities of political parties. However, the associa-tions constituted a much stronger institution than a political party. Each of the cultural associations in Vilafranca endured for decades; by contrast, since 1876, 115 political parties have appeared and disappeared in the Alto Panadés. Most of these parties vanished within three years of their founding (Sabaté i Mill 1966:4).

In Vilafranca the history of political parties was the same as anywhere else in Spain; my interviews suggest that no more than six militants had strong connections with political parties that were nationally prominent at a given historical moment. Once the party declined in national influence, and therefore in its ability to pay off its local clients, the association with which it was associated began to lose prestige and membership. The associations could survive (although not flourish) the ups and downs of political fortunes, but the parties themselves most often could not. But if the parties could not survive without the associations, neither could the as-sociations survive without political activities. The rise to promi-nence of each association, measured in terms of membership and social influence in the Alto Panadés, corresponds to the promi-nence in national politics of the leading members of the association. Thus the *casino* was most prominent when General Prim and his friends in the directorate of the *casino* represented the strongest political impulse in the *comarca*. The *centro* enjoyed its moment of glory when the monarchy was restored and consequently the interests of the rentiers closely linked with those of the central government. The *Sociedad la Principal* and the *ateneu* reached their apogee after the Catalan metropolitan bourgeoisie had begun to seek an accommodation with Madrid because of the growing threat of class conflict and had left Catalan nationalism to the popular classes.

Though it is clear that each association rose or fell according to the political prominence of its guiding spirit in a given historical moment, it is less clear how the same association could hold members of diverse political parties and social classes that were at war with one another nationally. According to all my informants, the critical element in maintaining the political coherence of the associations was the leaders of political parties, who vied with one another for office within the associations. This competition for office between the leaders of contending political parties was clearest in the epochs of electoral politics (1900–23, 1931–6). The leaders of the associations were often the *caciques* of one or another of the national parties. The prominence of the national party in part determined the prominence of the *cacique* on the local level. If his party was capable of winning an election, the party's followers were sure to gain the party's patronage, which was dispensed on the local level by the *cacique*. The system of *caciquismo* worked perfectly in Vilafranca del Panadés: In each of the seven elections to the national Cortes that took place between 1900 and 1917, the candidate favored by the *cacique* of the *Sociedad la Principal* won almost unanimously.[7]

The local *cacique* was far more than a vote deliverer for the national party and a patronage dispenser at the local level. To be a local *cacique*, a man had to be accepted by persons of all classes as a morally superior man. "The *cacique* was a man who took care of things for people" was the most common description given by my informants. He had to be able to unite all sorts of people, who were often in conflict with one another over political and economic matters. The principal talent of the *cacique* was his ability to excel in interpersonal relationships. Of a *cacique* who was a director of the *centro* in the 1890s, it is often said that people in the Alto Panadés were socially bestial until he taught them how to shake hands and speak to each other.[8]

In addition to rallying the populace for electoral politics, the *cacique* was supposed to set the intellectual and emotional tone of an association. He was supposed to be a sufficiently good orator to create a climate of opinion favorable to the endeavors of his party and to be well enough educated to discuss regionalist themes in the associations. For these reasons, professors from the local schools were often *caciques*.[9]

These local *caciques* and associational leaders created an idiom of comportment and discourse that contrasts strongly with the idiom of the bars that have replaced the associations in Vilafranca. In the associational millieu, the critical concept is embodied in one word, pregnant with meaning and almost untranslatable. That word is *seny*, which means in literal translation "judgment," "brains," or "common sense." *Seny* has, however, much wider meanings. It connotes a kind of virtue possessed by all Catalans when they compare themselves with the residents of non-Catalan regions of Spain. In this context, it means the commercial judgment and prudence of the entire Catalan population, as compared with the putative indolence and frivolity of other Spaniards. It encompasses the notion of formality in business dealings, the strict fulfillment of contractual obligations, and the honorable treatment of all people involved in economic production, from worker to businessman.

Seny has another and more restrictive meaning when it is applied by one Catlan speaking of another. Within the population of Catalans, only a few people really have *seny*. A person so described by a fellow Catalan is the repository of the above-cited virtues in the town or village where he lives. In the locality where a person lives, he is measured in terms of how he honors contracts, how he treats others, and so forth. There is no longer an abstract comparison between "foreigners" and "Catalans," but an absolute evaluation of a person's actions in face-to-face daily confrontations with others. In this restricted context, the danger of falling below standard is much greater than in the broader context. Businessmen cheat each other, landowners abuse their *rabassaires* or their factory workers and are curt and uncivil to many people. Daily life is filled with accusations and counteraccusations, gossip, lies, and intrigues. Everyone is subject to frailty and, in the light of constant scrutiny, also subject to wide variations in moral credit rating.

In the local context, a person described as having *seny* is almost superhuman, nearly free from the foibles of the population at large.

Many of the old association leaders are described as being endowed with *seny;* these men became leaders in part because their personalities transcended the ugly realities of the class struggle in the Alto Panadés. By personal moral force, a man like Clavé was able to bridge the gap between the bourgeoisie and the proletariat of Vilafranca del Panadés. Clavé embodied the ideal moral propensities of Catalan society of his day. By supplying culture to the workers he demonstrated that the bonds of Catalanism could be stronger than the bonds of social class. He was the living repository of Catalan regionalist ideology, a human showcase for the virtues of an entire people.

The somber mien of association members goes hand in hand with the ideal of *seny;* it is a business ethic, in which absolute sobriety is the proper way to live. Grave formality in interpersonal treatment bespeaks honor in business transactions; an atmosphere of frivolity suggests untrustworthiness in business. In sum, the cultural associations of the Alto Panadés provided idioms and opportunities for men of all classes, singly or in organized groups, to attempt to improve their economic and political conditions. The impetus for the creation of these institutions originally came from the industrial bourgeoisie in its attempt to control the countryside politically and economically in the mid-nineteenth century. But, at the end of the century, both the form of the associations and the emphasis on regional culture were taken over by the very classes the bourgeoisie had attempted to control.

Cultural associations and their attendant ideology of *seny* still exist in the Alto Panadés. All but the suppressed *ateneu* still have substantial membership composed of many people who were members before the advent of the Franco regime. But there are unmistakable signs that the associations are declining in vitality. First, young people do not seem interested in the associations save for participating in the weekend dances or athletics. They do not share their elders' commitment to Catalan regionalism and seem indifferent to the cultural and political aspects of the associations. Second, the ideological appeal of the associations excludes a large segment of the population of the *comarca* – the new working class, composed mainly of Castilians, who do not share the Catalan cultural tradition and therefore feel ideologically excluded from the associational milieu. In addition, most large landholders no longer frequent the associations and particularly not the *sociedad*, which is still the principal repository of Catalan regionalism. Finally, the central government has fostered political apathy in the Alto Panadés by systematic repression of the cultural associations. Though it is impossible to banish them entirely because they are the principal recreation centers of the *comarca*, local government officials maintain spies within the associations who keep their activities under constant surveillance. During my stay in the Alto Panadés, various programs involving Catalan folk drama and music were subject to censorship by the municipal officials. Overt political discussion is prohibited in the associations, and public discussion of the government is punished by fines for the individuals involved and general harassment of the association in which the discussion took place.

In short, the repression by the central government is progressively denaturing the associational life of Vilafranca. Though the repression is expressly aimed at the political component of the associations, particularly at celebrations of regionalism, it is also destroying the bases of civic action that regionalist politics generated and that produced the savings banks, medical organizations, pension funds, and insurance plans that benefited local citizens. Agencies of the state offer many of these same services, but the repression of the associations is inexorably undermining the spirit of Catalan unity that led the associations to create these services in the first place. Whatever sense of social commitment Catalans had is being eroded and replaced by a passive loyalty to the state, based on increasing and enforced dependency upon state agencies.

Despite the repression of the associations and the erosion of civic spirit in Vilafranca, one public forum is bursting with vitality. As the associations have waned, a thriving bar culture has increasingly provided the most dynamic locus of public intercourse in the Alto Panadés. Behind the hustle and bustle of the handful of fancy new bars in Vilafranca is the process of modernization. In the bars, those members of the bourgeoisie eager to enjoy the benefits of the government's modernization programs are searching for the clients necessary to the prosecution of their economic designs. A close study of the emergent bar culture sheds considerable light on modernization as a social experience as well as an economic process.

Bar scene on the Ramblas

Drinking to prosperity:
hedonism and modernization in Vilafranca

Although the programs and the power of the central government offer economic salvation and even increased prosperity to the Catalan bourgeoisie, the path to this prosperity is not without dilemmas. These dilemmas stem from the problematical relationships between the bourgeoisie and the government and between the bourgeoisie and the popular classes. The government views the Catalan bourgeoisie as a valuable economic asset but a political liability that cannot be allowed economic and political initiatives. The popular classes resent the bourgeoisie; the legacy of class hatred is still strong in the *comarca*, and the popular classes feel that the bourgeoisie has sold out Catalonia.

These complex and deep-seated hostilities cause serious problems for the bourgeois who wishes to modernize his farm or expand his business because his economic success depends upon entering into informal alliances with people from different social classes and with governmental officials as well. Faced with a stagnant vinicultural economy, frequently lacking the ability to farm, yet with a chance to take advantage of government programs and credits, the bourgeois must recruit strategic personnel to help him prosper. And strategic personnel consist of (1) government personnel attached to relevant state agencies and (2) members of the popular classes who possess relevant technical skills. Apart from the problem of social hostility, the bourgeois must compete for the services of these potential partners, for technical personnel are in short supply and can claim high prices both socially and economically, for their services and loyalties.

It is in this context that the bar culture of Vilafranca can best be understood. The characteristic social organization of the bar is the small-scale, informal coalition of eight to twenty men.[10] These coalitions generally consist of government officials, the bourgeoisie, small businessmen, and a wide variety of technicians, ranging from automobile mechanics to agrarian surveyors – persons representing the capital, skills, and power necessary for the modernization of agrarian estates. Such coalitions are forged and ruptured in the handful of fancy bars along Vilafranca's main thoroughfares.

All parties enter into such coalitions for instrumental reasons, principally to enrich themselves by claiming a piece of the action. Apart from personal enrichment, many individuals of working-class and petit bourgeois origins enter into them to gain social mobility. Despite the instrumentality of these relationships, the ritual and ideology of bar culture radically deemphasize the functional economic aspects of the coalitions. Factors such as personal wealth and/or professional skills, though essential to the existence and performance of the coalitions, are not overtly used to recruit membership. Additionally, no man can thoroughly succeed without a vast repertoire of social skills, which are generally put to use in the organization of the drinking and feasting activities of other men.

The bar culture is the very antithesis of the association culture. It is totally apolitical, totally committed to individual pursuits rather than collective goals, and ideologically devoted to hedonism rather than bourgeois prudence and sobriety. In fact, bar culture so wholeheartedly subscribes to the philosophy of "eat, drink and be merry" that the process of modernization in the Alto Panadés might well be described as a Rabelaisian movable feast.

The information presented in this section is based on intensive participant observation carried out in three of the six major bars in Vilafranca where the coalitions are formed and maintained. All these bars came to exist in their present form between 1959 and 1967, and all occupy prominent spots on the two main thoroughfares of Vilafranca. Their newness stands in stark contrast to the timeworn stolidity of the buildings that surround them. They physically resemble the fancy tourist bars of the nearby Mediterranean coast.[11] Since 1960, these few bars have become the most dynamic forums of public intercourse in the Alto Panadés, and bar culture has spread at the expense of the major voluntary associations that used to monopolize public recreation and intercourse.

Even to the most casual observer, these bars have an obvious dynamism, marked by the volume of people that pass their portals from as early as six in the morning to as late as six on the following morning. On weekdays, there is a continuous trickle of people from early morning to late afternoon, and by seven in the evening there is a veritable avalanche of patrons, who stay until just before the evening meal at ten. On Saturdays and Sundays, the flow of humanity is so great at all hours of the day that there is barely elbow room indoors and standing room only at the outdoor tables on the *ramblas*.

The bar's role as a center of communications is perhaps its most important. An essential part of this function entails keeping track of other people's whereabouts and doings. This sort of information is very useful in the Alto Panadés, since the economic pursuits of many people are diversified enough so that they do not remain in one place (e.g., an office) all day long. Even an efficient telephone system (which Vilafranca does not have) would not relieve the problem. The solution to finding people is to repair to the bar. If the person in question cannot be immediately located, the bartender takes a message for him. On an average day, a bartender takes well over 200 such messages, storing most of them in his head. The bar also serves as a gossip mill recording the activities of almost anyone in town. Discussing other people's activities and evaluating their characters is an essential of bar conversation. Far from being idle chatter, such conversations prove extremely useful in ferreting out news of coming economic possibilities and gaining insights about whom to ally with and whom to avoid. Such news and evaluations are absolutely essential in the drama of modernization in the Alto Panadés because people themselves are the resources in the process.[12]

The vital role of the bar in mediating human contacts has specialized importance for a certain type of small businessman. In Vilafranca, a number of men specialize in the sale of machinery, particularly agricultural machinery, but also automobiles and motor bikes. These men usually operate with precarious capitalization and a scarcity of goods. Rather than risk further capital by renting an office (which would isolate them from contacts anyhow), they simply circulate from bar to bar in search of customers. I recorded an interesting example. A young automobile salesman, Señor Llops, operated in this fashion to study the psychology of potential customers who were often unaware of their desire to purchase an automobile. Llops began his career as a garage mechanic; scraping together several weeks' earnings, he bought a second-hand motorcycle, reconditioned it, and sold it at a sufficient profit to buy two more motorcycles. In a few years, he had generated enough capital to move into the automobile business. As cars are costly in Spain, he must buy one and sell it before he can purchase another. Because his business is so small, he must actually guess who will be in the market for an auto and when. The logical marketplace is in the best bar in town, where he can measure psychologically the desires of affluent people for an auto. Through his understanding of the behavior appropriate to bar culture, he is able to meet and mix with all his potential clientele. Having ingratiated himself with a prospective buyer, Llops purchases a car he believes will interest his hoped-for client. He cleans and polishes the car and parks it in front of the potential customer's habitual bar. Almost always it is love at first sight between buyer and auto. Over a few hours of drinks, the deal is concluded, with a handsome profit for Llops. In the more than two years I observed him in action, he never failed to make a sale. Though few are so successful as Llops, such entrepreneurs abound in Vilafranca.

The principal social goals of participation in bar culture are to build new networks and maintain old ones. For the bourgeois with estates to modernize and for members of other social classes intent on social mobility, specific kinds of networks have to be cultivated that involve only specific people drawn from the various classes. From the perspective of the other classes and of government officials, the bourgeoisie has the lion's share of property, capital, and knowledge of economic opportunities in the *comarca*. Members of the haute bourgeoisie own the best agricultural land, the wineries, much real estate, factories; several have seats on the Barcelona stock exchange, and one owns a local bank as well as the most important bar. What lands and businesses they do not own are not worth owning, foreign-owned,[13] or government-owned. The bourgeoisie is thus in an excellent position to do favors for people less well endowed. Such favors can consist of taking a talented partner into an enterprise or merely furnishing information and influence to enable a person to set up business on his own.

From the perspective of the bourgeois, the modernization of his estate requires him to assemble, on an informal basis, a team of loyal dependents. Minimally he must be able to acquire the talents of various technicians: skilled agricultural workers; mechanics (to service the new machinery); machinery salesman (machines are still in short supply); experts on fertilizer, hybridization, and scientific cultivation. Additionally, if he is to take advantage of state aid to agriculture, he must deal on good terms with a wide range of government officials: bank officials from the Agrarian Credit Bank, technical personnel from the Agrarian Extension Service, provincial officials related to the viniculture cooperative, officials of the government labor syndicates. All these personnel are in short supply. In addition, each is at once a potential ally and a potential enemy: a potential ally in the sense that he could become a happy (dependent) partner in a prosperous business venture; a potential enemy in that his refusal or disaffection could cause serious reverses for the modernizing landowner.

The high stakes involved on all sides, the history of social conflicts, and the vagaries of informal coalition formation explain why personal prestige plays such an important role in the success or failure of individuals trying to reap the benefits of modernization. To succeed, an individual must live up to a complex code of good-fellowship. The playing out of this drama constitutes a great part of the bar culture and in itself is worthy of anthropological inquiry. To evaluate the role of prestige in bar culture, I have followed Silverman's (1966) variant of the reputational method, which stresses eliciting the criteria of prestige from the subjects themselves.

Eight informants were given a list of 100 names, 25 from each of the four major social classes of the *comarca* (haute bourgeoisie, petite bourgeoisie, workers, and *rabassaires*), and asked to rank each name according to the level of prestige its owner enjoyed in local society. The informants were then asked to explain their classification. Then each individual listed was discussed to ascertain how he fit the criteria defined by the informant. Informants' classifications were cross-checked by a number of simple card sorts done by other people and by direct observations of prestige-deference behavior in the local bars.

The object of the study was not just to classify individuals according to the prestige they enjoyed in local society. Because personal prestige is essential to individual success in getting into coalitions, an effort was made to crack the code of personal prestige as a necessary step to an understanding of coalition formation in the Alto Panadés. The magnitude of this problem for a foreign anthropologist can be readily understood when one considers that no Catalan entirely understands the code himself. Apart from presenting some of the results of prestige classification and their relationship to informal social organization, I can provide only a rough idea of the ideological component of the code of bar culture.

In the bar culture of Vilafranca, a person's prestige is a direct function of how well he is able to live up to the complex code of good-fellowship that mediates relationships between individuals. According to informants' criteria, the ability to get along with others *(relacionarse con otros, relacionarse con los demás)* far outweighs any other criterion of gaining prestige. Any discussion of a person's ability to get along with others automatically includes an analysis of the individual's personality; the key formula for such an analysis is: "*(X) tiene un carácter (cerrado, alegre, abierto, adusto,* etc.)" ("So and so has a [closed, happy, open, brusque, etc.] personality"). In turn, the strength of an individual's personality is the key to his success (or lack of it) in attaining prestige and is a crucial factor in his ability to claim a spot in one of the coalitions.

Personality is viewed locally as a multifaceted entity, just as being able to get along with others is viewed as a complex process. Judgments about the nature of a man's personality are filtered through at least four major cultural constructs long familiar to students of Hispanic society: *cultura, gracia, simpatía,* and *honra.* The first refers to the upbringing of the individual, his breeding;

the second is a quality of the essential personality and refers to charm and wit; the third refers to the quality of empathizing with others and evoking empathy in return; and the fourth refers to a person's ability to protect his familial and personal reputation from the depredations of immoral individuals and from abusive encroachments by diverse authority figures (e.g., bosses, the government). These four concepts hang together like a constellation, and failure to develop them successfully is reflected in diminished prestige, which in turn reduces the range of social action an individual enjoys.

The importance of these concepts is further highlighted by informants' evaluations of some of the more spectacular social failures in Vilafranca. Six individuals were ranked at the bottom of the prestige hierarchy for being given over to vice *("entregado al vicio")*. Two were homosexuals, one a prostitute (the only one in the town), one too devoted to the pleasures of Barcelona whorehouses *("demasiado putero")*, and two incorrigible drunks.[14] Failure of this sort is viewed as a serious deficiency in breeding *("gran falta de cultura")*. Such deficiencies in breeding lead to the dimunition of honor as well, rendering such individuals outside the boundaries of normal social intercourse.

Far more serious personality deficiencies derive from abuse of power, which is viewed as stemming from wealth, political position, or both. Abuse of power is not viewed as an abstract matter, but as something that can occur in the context of dyadic relationships, man to man. The mere possession of public office in an area hostile to the central government is sufficient to engender a host of anecdotes relating to the abuse of power. Thus the mayor of the town, an able administrator cursed with a dour personality, was placed at or near the bottom of the hierarchy by all my informants and described by one as "the ideal chief of a Nazi concentration camp" *("el jefe perfecto de un campo de concentración nazi")*. A working-class man who had risen to the post of councilman in the municipal government was even more rigorously downgraded than the mayor. He had arbitrarily instituted a system of alternate-side-of-the-street parking in Vilafranca, causing great inconvenience to the auto owners of the town. For this, he is shunned on the street and has received the nickname Don Disco (Mr. Parking Sign); it is reputed that "he even hangs those signs on his mother's balls" *("hasta los cojones de su madre cuelga discos")*.

Abuses of power stemming from disparities in wealth are much more common than abuses deriving from the exercise of public office. The owner of a business can lose his prestige either by attempting to exact extraordinary services from his employees or by issuing commands to an employee that the latter considers degrading. Such commands or extraordinary services always have to be refused with great dramatic vigor, at least in the recounting of the incident to a foreign anthropologist. Minimally, negation of the demand involves an emphatic, "No, Señor," followed by the resignation of the employee on the spot. Various informants stressed that not only had they refused and resigned, but they had also had their revenge, including physical reprisals.[15] Such abuses are felt to constitute a direct affront to personal honor, which is precarious and must be maintained at all costs. As the abuse of power in this fashion could potentially occur in any situation where there is a disparity in wealth between partners, bar culture comes to stress a nearly exaggerated courtesy between such people.

In addition to the major social sins and personality defects discussed above, informants provided me with a catalog of less grievous, but still significant, social sins that have a direct bearing on bar culture. All these sins have ambiguous qualities, but ambiguity is part of any prestige-deference system. The first sin is to be pretentious or presumptuous (*presumido*), to pretend to be more than one actually is. The second is interfering in the affairs of others (*metirse*). The third is being overconcerned with one's economic affairs (*siempre al negocio*). The ambiguity stems from the fact that bar culture involves doing all three of these things as vigorously as possible. The people who fail to attain the upper reaches of the prestige hierarchy are those who do these necessary operations in bad style. Acquiring the proper style becomes a life-long preoccupation for participants in bar culture, and the statistical probabilities of personal success are stacked against them.

What kind of behavior is associated with the prestige code in the context of bar culture? The demonstration of good-fellowship involves spending a great deal of time, money, and effort buying drinks for one's cohorts at local bars and organizing impromptu suppers for them in a variety of regional restaurants. Success in the demonstration of good-fellowship is contingent on having a solid physical constitution, because eating and drinking are done in heroic proportions, repetitively and at irregular hours. Absenting oneself from the bar for several days brings complaints from companions of inattention to their primary needs. The stress on eating and drinking has evolved into an ideology in which hedonism is a reciprocal of ingestion. The organization of action invariably begins with statements such as: "We've got to go to bar *X* to drink Priorato wine." "Let's go to restaurant *Y* to get some of those octopuses." "A fine afternoon like today means we can drive over to Casa Marisco for those special prawns." Regardless of the hour, a gustatory excursion for eight to twenty persons is organized within five minutes. On two occasions within five years, this ideology led to the development of a quasiformal men's supper club, with membership of about fifty.

The proper atmosphere for these activities is one of enforced jollity; everyone must appear to be amusing himself to the utmost, without a care in the world *(sin preocupaciones)*. Anyone appearing momentarily preoccupied is gently prodded by his companions, who inevitably ask: "Why are you so serious, man?" *("¡Hombre! ¿Porqué tan serio?")* Anyone wishing to start a somewhat serious conversation is reminded: "But we are here to amuse ourselves, don't be such a bore" *("Estamos aquí para divertirnos, no seas tan pesado")*. Should the immediate realities of food and drink not be sufficient to amuse those present, then either joking (each group inevitably seems to contain one joker) or singing will fill the void. Judged by its atmosphere, bar culture appears to involve a certain amount of just plain frivolity.

Nothing could be further from the truth in terms of social outcomes, however. Minimally, the emphasis on pleasures of the moment allows people who are suspicious of each other for any of the reasons outlined earlier in this chapter to suspend traditional judgments, as a prelude to becoming friends and allies or, if such relationships have already been achieved, to maintaining them. It allows them also to avoid considering the impact of the social changes their alliance will bring about in the *comarca*. As the directions of such changes have been hotly contested in recent history, the functional advantages of such a code are obvious. All are striving to enrich themselves as individuals, not as representatives of any identifiable social group. In the code of good-fellowship, society is blurred in a haze of alcohol and a whiff of garlic. Both were always important in local society, but they have not heretofore served to sublimate its realities.

A more mundane consideration also explains the premiums placed on *gracia, cultura, simpatía,* and general good-fellowship. The bars, as I have described above, serve as clearinghouses for all manner of small businesses in the Alto Panadés. Because the business situation is at once small-scale and fluid, men often have to wait for long periods at the bars to make contacts. There is a need to while away the waiting time, to alleviate the boredom of waiting and the tiring repetitiveness of cementing one's interpersonal relationships with hours of social drinking. In such circumstances, an entertainer is a godsend. A person can, with jokes, songs, and conviviality, make his hearers forget the repetitiveness of their life circumstances and the precariousness of their social and economic standing. By lightening the spirits of all present, the wit or the comic may also enhance his own business interests. A fine example is the car salesman, Señor Llops. Llops has a huge amount of animal vitality; he is proud that he is more of a glutton for food and drink than even the most prosperous men of the *comarca,* that he is always the first to form an impromptu party and to sponsor a quick foray to Sitges or Barcelona. When conversation lags at the bar, Llops uses his fine baritone voice to belt out old regional and new popular songs. Shortly, everyone joins in, and the singing usually continues until the small hours of the morning, improving as vocal cords are loosened with champagne. When everyone else is sagging from food, drink, and plain exhaustion, Llops is as bright-eyed as he was at midday and ready to continue the battle indefinitely. Apart from entertaining his friends, Llops has simultaneously laid the groundwork for new business transactions and shored up old friendships. As business transactions are completed only after friendships are established, Llops' virtuoso performance is rooted in sound business principles.

Whereas the code of the bar culture stresses individualism, it also stresses a kind of egalitarianism that suppresses overt differences of social class. Anyone can enter a bar and seek companionship; participation in bar culture is one of the few democratic aspects remaining in local life. The stress on succeeding by dint of individual personality reinforces this kind of democracy and levels social claims based on inequalities in wealth and power. There are subtleties to this facet of bar culture that were brought to my attention by both informants and casual discussants. For example, since the advent of bar culture and the possibilities of modernization, the more clever wealthy bourgeoisie have begun to dress more humbly; today they wear the pants and shirts of clerks and workers, whereas fifteen years ago all wore suits.[16] And in spite of their wealth, many purchase small autos, such as the Citroen Deux Cheveaux or SEAT coupé, instead of the Rolls Royce they would have bought only a short while ago. One working-class informant commented on this trend by stating in exasperation: *"Ni saben ser ricos"* ("They don't even know how to be rich").

Once the stylistic nuances of the code of good-fellowship have been mastered to some degree, the business of serious coalition formation can take place: Alliances can be successfully forged between previously unaffiliated individuals. Yet the development of substantive relationships depends upon the ability to continuously demonstrate one final aspect of the code. Although this is often left unstated, it is certainly implied in informants' statements that success in both achieving prestige and making alliance depends upon an individual's ability *to perform favors for others*. This can be attempted gracefully only *after* a person has established himself according to the criteria discussed above.

Doing favors in the Alto Panadés consists of having the knowledge and connections to intervene decisively and favorably in the life problems of others, great and small. The range of favors done in this context is far too great to be detailed here: Some examples are illustrative. *"Me hizo el gran favor de ———"* ("He did me the favor of ———") is the stock phrase used to describe everything from fixing a traffic ticket of Don Disco's to making a government official a consultant to a company. It includes things like providing transportation for those who need it, being able to intervene with officials over pending legal matters, providing introductions for people in need of contacts generally, getting the best deal for a friend at a shop, and providing useful information about pending business deals before they are known to the general public. None of these examples is idiosyncratic; such favors are recorded again and again in my notes and I have often observed them as a participant.[17] But doing favors in isolated incidents is not sufficient to guarantee high prestige; everyone does this to a greater or lesser extent. The most prestigious individual is able to do such favors consistently, and gracefully, so that the recipient can never be seen as a dependent of the donor.

The obstacles to success in the bar culture are legion. For persons whose economic activities are so diverse and far flung as to necessitate much traveling, absence prevents the required good-fellowship. Local hostilities impede the success of many, and others are the victims of schemes that were improbable in the first place. There are in fact a number of highly successful individuals, but the life trajectories of most are at best erratic.[18]

We can now turn to the actual prestige classification of the 100 individuals in the sample and try to explain the results. The statistical results are displayed in the accompanying table. I have followed the informants' ranking system closely as to the number of categories and the classification of individuals,[19] but it is necessary to make explicit what is only implicit in many of their explanations of local prestige hierarchies. What is readily apparent but emphatically denied by the code is that only members of the haute bourgeoisie can become *"gente de primera categoría"* ("first-class people"). Though very few of the haute bourgeoisie were categorized as first class, nobody else was even considered for this category. It is significant that the six men at the apex of the prestige hierarchy were also those who stood at the apex of the coalitions in the bars. All these men were heavily committed to the modernization of their estates and were involved in many other business ventures as well, so that they were ideally placed to do favors for clients in search of a patron. All had considerable social skills and

Prestige classification of 100 men sampled in study of bar culture in Vilafranca

Social class[a]	Prestige category				
	1	2	3	4	Total
Haute bourgeoisie	6	16	3	0	25
Petite bourgeoisie	0	14	11	0	25
Workers	0	10	11	4	25
Rabassaires	0	0	10	15	25
Total	6	40	35	19	100

[a] Social class is here defined in standard political economic terms. For a full account of local class structure, see Hansen (1969).

amazing energy, much of which was poured into the bar culture, building and maintaining ties of loyalty and dependence.

Most men in Vilafranca believe that members of the wealthy bourgeoisie are ideally "doers of favors." When they do them consistently, gracefully, and publicly, they rise in the local prestige hierarchy. The converse is also true, as illustrated by the three bourgeois classed as third rate. These three men were so wealthy and powerful that they needed no dependents locally. All had the deserved reputation of doing nothing for others. The rage against them for this neglect was apparent in the informants' tales about these men. For example, one was reputed to amuse himself by humiliating the workers at his factory by taking them to lunch in fancy restaurants, even though they were dressed in their working clothes. Another cared so little about local society that he was reputed to associate only with Americans and Germans at a ritzy Barcelona golf club. Such stories may be fanciful, but they underlie the popular expectations of generosity from the wealthy.

Second-class people, those described as *"normal y correcto"* ("normal and correct"), come from three different social classes. Included are minor patrons from the haute bourgeoisie and successful clients recruited from the petite bourgeoisie and the workers. These men are all well liked and respected, but lack the social vigor and generally the economic power of those ranked first class. They are commonly described as having the continued ability *"relacionarse con gente de primera categoría"* ("to have relations with first-class people"). It is noteworthy that no *rabassaire* was placed in this grouping; modernization of estates means the elimination of the *rabassaires* as a social class and, consequently, their ineligibility for clienthood in bar culture. It is rare to see a sharecropper in the bars, and few of them are known to the bar habitués.

Third-class people, those described as *"normal y corriente"* ("normal and ordinary"), seem generally to be failed clients in search of a patron, although there is a small number of antisocial haute bourgeoisie in this category as well. These third-rate people are hangers-on in the bars. Many have a history of defaulting on their obligations to others, and some are downgraded for character defects that lead them to violate the code. Several are newcomers to the area, who have not yet learned how to manipulate the code. In short, people in this category have at least one outstanding social defect, but are still in the running for client positions within the coalitions.

The fourth-class is my own creation, based on implicit evidence supplied by informants about people who were known either not at all or not very well. Such men did not frequent the bars, out of choice or out of fear. Not to be known in Vilafranca is to be suspected of gross character defects, to become a "nonperson." Such people were consistently referred to by informants as lacking in either sufficient "category" or "balls" to get along with other people *("no tiene la categoría [los huevos] sufficiente[s] para relacionarse con la gente")*. Apart from bestowing a profoundly negative rating in the prestige hierarchy, such statements underline the tensions involved in bar culture, which is seen as a contest where one's manhood is on the line. In a situation where people themselves are resources, withholding oneself is the most sublime but the most difficult of social skills. Subsequent interviews with people classified as fourth rate revealed that many find the social climbing in the bars repugnant. In their view, the bars are the places where the "rich and presumptuous" *("los ricos y presumidos")* make fools of themselves publicly.

One more implicit prestige category was suggested by several informants who were attempting to connect the prestige system of the Alto Panadés to one that was nationwide. The informants who were concerned about this stated that Vilafranca did not *really* have any first-class people because no one from the *comarca* was a national figure, such as a prominent politician or an economic titan. They stressed that this was a recent development, that before the civil war there had been seven or eight individuals who were nationally known and whose portraits still hang in the Gallery of Illustrious Vilafrancans in the town hall. Their concern underlines the fact that people in Vilafranca (and elsewhere in rural Catalonia) have no real power on a national level and little leverage in the process of modernization that is so dramatically changing the *comarca*.

This lack of power and control over the process of social change in the Alto Panadés goes a long way toward explaining the precarious nature of both individual prestige and the coalitions themselves. As no one in the *comarca* is involved in the decision-making process that formulates the major outlines of modernization, local strategies can only be reactive and speculative to whatever is de-

creed from above. As conditions are always in flux, the requirements for instrumental relationships on the part of the local
bourgeoisie can change quickly, closing off avenues of mobility for
some old allies and creating chances for new ones. This process
probably lies behind the many stories of interpersonal treason that
make up bar culture. It also may inhibit the size of coalitions that
can be constructed, which generally include no more than twenty
people.

6

The faces of power in the Alto Panadés

It should by now be obvious that the facts of power have much to do with decline of regional culture. We turn, therefore, to analyze some of the ways power is wielded in the Alto Panadés, by whom, and for whose benefit. Because power is always wielded at somebody's expense in favor of somebody else's interests, we also want to know whose interests are thwarted by the government, and why this is so. Just as we want to know who gets the rewards offered by this type of government, we also want to know who is suffering from political repression and who is excluded from economic opportunities.

This account is limited in certain critical ways because of the nature of the research itself and because of the political climate in which it was done. A thorough study of the many ways in which power is organized in the *comarca* would require, among other things, some formal considerations about the decision-making processes in key ministries like economy and agriculture. In these ministries, policies relating to agrarian credits, reforms, and tariffs are worked out, and the machinery to implement these policies is developed. Additionally, attention would have to be paid to the problems of regional-level administrations in adjusting these policies to fit regional economic and political conditions – problems especially great in a hostile region like Catalonia. Clearly, the citizens of the Alto Panadés or of Catalonia are not privy to the decision-making processes, and neither is the anthropologist living among them. To comprehend these macrostructures, we have to resort to abstract models such as those of Linz (1962).

Even at the local level (in this case *comarcal*), not all the fields of power are readily accessible either to the citizenry or to a social scientist, although both are thoroughly enmeshed in them. In a Catalan *comarca*, a foreign anthropologist who consorted freely with representatives of the state might well find himself excluded

134

from social relationships with everyone else who lived there: The officials of the central government are not the most highly regarded people in the Alto Panadés. Reliance on such individuals as the sole informants about local realities would result in an essay in science fiction, not social science.

Despite these limitations, there are some valid approaches to the study of power in small locales such as the Alto Panadés. One approach is to account for the way the people who live there perceive the political process and their varied roles in it. The best anthropological work is that which discusses the quality of life diverse peoples endure and/or enjoy. A cardinal theme of twentieth-century anthropological research must be the way the expansion of state power has affected the quality of life everywhere in the world by abolishing localisms and individual freedoms. Viewed in these terms, a political account of life in the Alto Panadés is a description of how some individuals embrace social deracination in order to stay afloat economically, and the remainder are caught up in the unfolding of an Orwellian drama. In this context, the realities of power in the Alto Panadés become to some extent transcendental; they become a paradigm for what happens to people caught up in the extraordinary expansion of state power that has occurred since World War II.

But in Spain state expansion has not yet gone so far that no initiative can be generated at local levels, although none can be attempted that requires local-level mobilization. The initiatives, economic and political, of the state are the most dynamic and powerful in the nation at present, but the Spanish state is in no position to guarantee that its policies will be implemented to the fullest in every part of the land, just as it cannot guarantee that its laws will be obeyed to the letter in every region. Not only does the government lack sufficient administrative density and armed force to do this, but as Wolf (1959) pointed out for sixteenth-century Mexico, life is simply too protean to be perfectly contained by laws and policies. Thus, opportunities are created in each locale by the state, but it is up to individuals to make the most of these opportunities. This chapter discusses how the opportunities are created, what strategies are required to realize them, and what kinds of initiatives are thwarted.

In the Alto Panadés the central government operates on two levels: (1) the repression of political life and (2) the implementation of national economic policies. Different clusters of governmental agencies, staffed by different types of personnel, are charged with carrying out the will of the central government on these two levels. Repression is primarily the responsibility of the high-ranking officials of the municipal government *(ayuntamiento)*, who are backed up by the rural political police force *(guardia civil)*. Economic policies are executed by diverse governmental agencies, among them banks, the National Wheat Service (the government's wheat monopoly), the Agrarian Extension Service (a technical aide to agriculture), and the various syndical organizations. Key officials in charge of political repression have generally been recruited from the Alto Panadés, and particularly from Vilafranca. The notable exception is the *guardia civil* contingent, whose composition is primarily Castilian and Andalusian. Technical agencies are also generally staffed by nonlocal people, although many are Catalans from other districts. These technical personnel are recruited on the basis of occupational skills.

The structure of repression and the politics of apathy

At present, repression is largely a matter of harassment and fines levied against anyone deemed to be engaging in unauthorized political activities. A small contingent of tommy-gun-bearing police,[1] twelve men for the entire district, is the sole symbol of the government's coercive powers, although until 1964, Vilafranca was garrisoned by 500 troops from the regular Spanish Army. The daily routines of the *guardia civil* consists mainly of surveillance, conducted often on foot throughout the Alto Panadés. Surveillance is carried out principally by contacting the mayors of the towns and villages and asking for information about local activities and people. The *guardia's* business is to know who lives where and what they do; usually the police attempt to interview informally anyone who moves into the Alto Panadés.[2] At present, the *guardia* uses this information network principally to investigate nonpolitical crimes, such as murder and rape or criminal insanity.[3] In addition, it assists in handling major traffic problems and highway accidents on national and provincial highways throughout the district.

It is important to note that the *guardia civil*, an agency of the national government, handles all important police functions at the local level. Nothing is left to the municipal police, save directing local traffic and assisting drunks on their way home. The local police are considered buffoons, whose jobs are classic examples of *ayuntamiento* sinecures. In contrast, the *guardia civil* is viewed with a mixture of fear and respect, as an alien occupying force. Viewed in another light, the *guardia* might be simply the armed guarantor of public apathy.

Less visible than the *guardia civil*, the most active agents of the repression are the high-ranking officials of the Vilafranca *ayuntamiento*, in particular the mayor and the secretary. These officials are dedicated to stamping out all extralegal political activity. It is they who deny permits to groups wishing to hold assemblies, and it is they who levy the fines for illegal assembly and real or assumed insults to the regime, verbal or printed.

No one could accuse the incumbents of sloth in the prosecution of their tasks; their zeal seems occasionally to border on insanity. Apart from their rigorous harassment of the cultural associations, they insist on hearing the lyrics of folk songs before they are sung and place a heavy fine on such a minor infraction as mailing post-cards celebrating the fact that the regime had allowed spring to arrive on time. This unstinting harassment assumes the proportions of a crusade, with the objective of exorcising the demon of politics from the bosom of the local citizenry.

There is a structural basis for the fervor of repression at the local level: Both the mayor and the secretary lack tenure of office; they can be replaced for any reason at all by the civil governor of Barcelona, the highest ranking official of the province of Barcelona. It is a widely held view among the citizens of Vilafranca that this lack of tenure causes the mayor to be "more dictator than Franco himself." Fearing for their jobs, the mayor and the secretary carry out to the letter of the law what they imagine to be the dictates of the central government.

The fact that the mayor's office carries out the real political dirty work of the government has an interesting ideological consequence among the citizenry. Popular discontent has a local focus—the *ayuntamiento* and its personalities—rather than the national government. In 1967 the central government, save for those citizens with some political sagacity and the local elite, was viewed as the personality of Franco, not as an organized political entity with diverse organisms. The most universal sentiment, shared by all classes equally, was that Franco was a dictator and a dictatorship is a bad thing, but that he was an honorable man who brought the nation "peace and tranquility." Therefore, everyone feared his death, and prayed he would live a thousand years.

The attitude toward the mayor is quite otherwise: There was considerable rejoicing when a wayward firecracker blew off part of his cheek on Saint Felix's Day in 1967.[4] Hence, the institutional workings of government are frequently obscured on a popular level by a focus on personalities; it is not that the mayor is fulfilling his obligations, but rather that the mayor is a bastard. Franco, in the remoteness of his official personality, seemed a saint by comparison.

Who are the men at city hall in the Alto Panadés? What segment of the local population do they represent? What sort of men are willing to suffer popular disapproval in various forms by overtly casting their loyalties with the central government? Insight into the operations of the regime at local levels can be gained from answering these questions. During the course of fieldwork, I expended considerable effort to get biographical information on men who had held high posts in the *ayuntamientos* of the Alto Panadés. Particular attention was focused on the positions of mayor and secretary; some consideration was given to men who had held (or held) the post of town councilman. More weight was given to the mayor and secretary, because they hold the whip hand in the politics of repression. The councilmen, along with the mayor and secretary, exercise their official capacities primarily in local matters: figuring out how best to collect the garbage or repair the streets. However, by association with the regime through the *ayuntamiento*, they have sometimes to endure popular censure. I assumed that if they were willing to endure this type of censure, their loyalty to the regime merited some consideration.

A discussion of the powers of local officials has to be centered upon Vilafranca del Panadés, the sole adminsitrative center in the *comarca*. Scarcely a drop of power is allocated to the twenty-one villages in the Alto Panadés. The only village official of any consequence is the mayor, whose position is largely ceremonial, owing to lack of funds and power to undertake public projects. In one village, the sole municipal function demanding the attention of the mayor was to find someone to weed the local cemetery. In principle, however, the mayor can exert considerable negative power over the lives of certain individuals residing in his village, as he serves as the principal character witness to the *guardia civil* for all his villagers. At the end of the civil war, quite a number of Falangists became village mayors and informed against the supporters of the fallen republic. Since the end of World War II, however, village mayors have tended to be the largest landholders in the vicinity and to have little or no power.

High-ranking posts in the *ayuntamiento* of Vilafranca are held by men with substantial properties and prestige occupations. The lesser post of councilman shows more variation; working-class men have occasionally held this position, as have many small shopkeepers. Councilmen come from a variety of social classes because the post is actually remote from power; the council is generally a rubber stamp for the high-ranking officers, who usually pick its members.[5] However, to suggest that leadership posts automatically fall to members of certain social positions would be misleading. Criteria other than social class are perhaps decisive in determining who will man the heights of local political power.

To understand the local leadership structure, we need to apply Linz's (1962:296–7) concept of "limited pluralism." The term refers to the fact that various group interests can participate in the government; that is, the regime is not a political monolith. Many political, status, and interest groups support the regime and are, in turn, acceptable to it.[6] In the Alto Panadés, identifiable groups of this sort include the *Falangists*, the Catholic action groups, high-status professionals (e.g., lawyers and doctors), financiers, and substantial proprietors. Perhaps it would be justified to add men's crony groups as a principal subdivision of the above-named groups. There is a marked tendency for groups of close friends to appear in the *ayuntamiento* at the same time.[7]

Each of these groups has a constituency, whether formally organized or not. How well a group is able to represent its constituency, I am not sure. For example, when a lieutenant mayor comes from a Catholic action group, I am not sure exactly how much influence this group can assert in the *ayuntamiento*. Consultation with members of these groups left me with a strong impression that such influence is actually minimized by the mayor and the secretary. Various bitter complaints along these lines suggest that the mayor uses his power to co-opt representatives of the diverse groups on issues of possible political import, but further research is necessary to clarify this point.

Some light can be thrown on this problem by employing Linz's (1962:301) concept of "mentality" as opposed to "ideology." He defines mentality as "ways of thinking or feeling, related to the present or past" and ideology as "an intellectually organized system of thought with a strong utopian element." Viewed in the Spanish historical context, these two concepts are antithetical, as ideology is a metaphor for the "political" past, and mentality for the "apolitical" present. The mentalities of most of the men who occupy public office in the Alto Panadés were formed in the crucible of political life as it existed prior to 1939. They view the turbulence of that political life as distinguished by excesses committed in the name of ideology (utopia). Not only do most of them abhor ideology, but many show an aversion to new ideas. A few have gone so far that they cannot even approve of thinking. The Spanish government does not like either intellectuality or politics. A free flow of thought and action is anathema to it and to those who serve it.

Nevertheless, most of the people who have occupied posts in the apparatus of repression are not stupid, vindictive, or socially anomalous (although some have managed to show all three of these traits). In fact, they represent the fears all people feel when the established order is threatened, as Spain's was by revolution less than two generations ago. It is not only fear of loss of property and social position, but fear of loss of life and fear of the *random* violence that occurred when public order collapsed in 1936. It is a fear that merges the dread of the social pathologies unleashed by the collapse of public order with anxiety about the direction of social change brought about by popular political action. The political crystallization of this fear is an overwhelming concern with law and order on the part of government officials, which was echoed by the local population in their concern for General Franco's longevity.

Thus, although many of the officials in the municipal government since 1939 have been at least technically members of the pre–civil war Spanish Right (e.g., Falangists, members of the Catholic action group, Monarchists), most have little political background. The vast majority held no public office prior to the war and profess not to have been adherents to, much less leaders of, any political party or faction in the prewar era. Many seem to be simple parochial conservatives, or as they are sometimes called "men of the town square," a term that denotes the narrow limits of their life experiences and the provincialism of their social visions.

Most are also older men, who were already young adults by the time of the civil war and whose political thinking has been shaped almost entirely by that terrible event.

Señor Barriga, now a lieutenant mayor of the *ayuntamiento*, illustrates this kind of mentality. He is in his late fifties. He has inherited substantial commercial and agricultural properties. Though he sympathized with the Nationalists in the civil war, he never joined any party and disclaims interest in doing so. He belongs to various associations, but has never held any position of leadership in them, by personal preference. He is, however, a leading figure and honorary officer of one of the men's eating and drinking groups. His main pleasures are those of a man about town; he loves bars and light conversation, and is well liked by all. When the mayor requested that Señor Barriga serve a term as lieutenant mayor, he at first refused, confiding to friends that he felt such a position would jeopardize his popularity in bars and clubs. However, the mayor persisted (Barriga claims he was actually dragooned into the position), and Barriga became an unwilling public servant. Several months passed, and Barriga had made no earth-shaking decisions, but had marched in several religious festival parades as a representative of the *ayuntamiento*. When chided during a bar conversation about his affiliation with city hall and the evil mayor, Barriga said sadly but doggedly, "We of the generation of the war feel that way." It is this mentality, rather than a fixed ideological stance, that dominates the high-ranking officials of city hall. In fact, it can be argued that an ideological disposition or strong participation in any of the war era parties is likely to keep a person from ascension to power in the municipal government. Some large property holders have never been asked to join the *ayuntamiento* because of past affiliation with the *Lliga Regionalista* or present affiliation with *Opus Dei*.[8] The same is true for members of the *Falange*, the official party of the state modeled after the Italian Fascist party. Whereas all members of any *ayuntamiento* are technically considered to be Falangists, almost no one has a firm commitment to the ideological precepts of the party, and it is doubtful that most even own the blue shirt that is required wear at party functions. Given the postwar decline of the party (principally a result of the Franco regime's deemphasis of the national political role of the *Falange* and its Castilian character, the *Falange* has few Catalan adepts. The handful of members in the Alto Panadés who still embrace its ideological tenets are viewed as political dinosaurs by the average citizen and as possible sources of embarrassment by those who wield power.

In fine, few men who have served in the *ayuntamiento* can be said to have pursued political careers. In the administration in office at the time this research was done only the mayor and the secretary were political figures. The remaining public officials – the councilmen and the lieutenant mayors – were representatives of the depoliticization carried out by the Franco regime. The importance of these men lies not so much in the power they wield (the mayor and the secretary have the real official power to carry out the repression), but in the personal prestige they lend the local government. As most men selected by the mayor for public office have distinguished themselves in some way, their presence in the administration cannot help but give a measure of popular legitimacy to the *ayuntamiento* and, by extension, to the repression itself.

In attempting to analyze the structure and effects of the repression on local life, it would be a mistake to concentrate on the aspects of it that are carried out by force alone. Although the force of the state is, of course, essential to maintaining the repression, the growth of public political apathy is the most profound consequence of the regime's efforts in the Alto Panadés. Gone are the days of the political exile, the garrisoning of the town by the regular army, and the closing of the *Ateneu Obrer*. Today, the fruits of this kind of repression are being reaped in the form of popular indifference toward "politics."

Political apathy is spread out through all segments of the population, but is especially marked in three important social groupings: Castilian workers, the bourgeoisie, and youth (regardless of class background). The apathy of the first two groups is relatively easy to explain. Castilian workers are fairly new arrivals to the area, refugees from the poverty of south and central Spain. Lacking both social roots in the area and a Catalan cultural background, they are unlikely candidates for membership in the associations and are immune to popular Catalanism. Additionally, they earn high wages (especially compared with wages in the areas they come from) and are much more concerned with using their newfound wealth to better their life circumstances than they are with politics. As their continued good fortune depends upon ingratiating themselves with a Catalan bourgeois patron, who in turn is beholden to the government for his very survival, any interest in politics would be deterimental to success.

Political apathy among members of the local bourgeoisie is a structural requirement of their economic position. Were it not for the victory of the Franco regime in the civil war, they would not even own their properties in the Alto Panadés. On top of this obvious debt of gratitude, they are increasingly dependent upon the state to further enhance their economic position by state credits and expansion of state technical services. Although they are excluded from major national policy decisions that directly affect them, their political silence at least guarantees their prosperity. Once the staunchest advocates of "Catalonia for the Catalans," they are now the first to denounce the excesses of a free political life.

Explaining the apathy of young people (between the ages of sixteen and thirty) is much more complicated and can be approached only superficially here. Young people generally show little interest in creating or joining any political party and are no more than moderately interested in the associational life that continues to be so vital to their fathers. It is almost impossible for them to analyze the political and economic life of the nation or even of the Alto Panadés, as they lack the political frames of reference that inform the views of their elders on these matters.

The difference in the political thinking of the generations cannot be overemphasized in the light of the history of the Alto Panadés. Until the Franco regime, every adult was brought up with some political vision of the world and how best to act upon it. To an American anthropologist, used to the low level of popular political consciousness at home, the grasp of political concepts and strategies among rather ordinary rural Catalans was a revelation. Thinking that political economy was something one learned in college, I was amazed at the way older workers and sharecroppers were able to give lucid Marxist accounts of their condition. Among older petit bourgeois individuals and landholders, I listened to elegant formulations of popular Catalanism and conservative regionalist philosophy. All political tendencies of the past still had their articulate, living exponents in the Alto Panadés.

The political muteness of the young stands in sharp contrast to the sophistication of their elders. It can be explained partly by the fact that, in contrast to their elders, the young have grown up in an atmosphere of no political life whatsoever. They have also been subjected to a barrage of government propaganda throughout their school careers, and they have been confronted with the distractions of a consumer economy and tourism. All these forces operating simultaneously produced a generation with precious little social commitment to community or nation. In lieu of the social and political commitments of their parents, the young are concerned with living the good life modernization provides. Rather than listen to some old man recounting the greater glory of Catalonia at one of the associations, they prefer to hang out at the tourist bars on the coast. To them the good life consists of dressing well, enjoying TV and hard rock music, and achieving some degree of emancipation from their parents. It is interesting that almost none of the things in vogue with the young is Spanish or Catalan; youth culture is based heavily on foreign models, particularly American and British.

It is not only in the young, the bourgeoisie, and the Castilian workers that political apathy has taken root. The flourishing bar culture is, as we have seen in Chapter 5, a creation of both de-politicization and economic transformation. Adults and young adults from all social origins devote an increasing amount of time to participating in this milieu, at the expense of time invested in the associations. Although part of the lure of the bars is their modern-ity, their principal social feature is the informal grouping of self-interested contact building that goes on there. The associations have always tried to encourage collective action on pressing social problems; in the bars, only individuals are important. One of the consequences of repression is the atomization of social life into individual scramblings for prestige and wealth.

Although the central government, through its local organs of repression, has succeeded in disengaging most people in the Alto Panadés from the political process, new forms of opposition are evolving. Most interesting is the increasing resistance of the lower clergy of the Catholic church to the national government in general and to the repression specifically. This resistance seems anomalous on two counts: (1) the church is officially one of the pillars of the central regime, a fact the church hierarchy seems very proud of; and (2) the ideology exposed by these visionary young priests has a strong Marxist component, and priestly references to the class struggle are nearly as common as references to the Savior. In Vila-franca the principal organization of the young priests is the Young

Catholic Workers movement, which, although small in membership, is increasingly affecting the lives of young people.

It would be unwise to present data on the harassment of the Young Catholic Workers,[9] but it is pertinent to sketch the positions of this organization that are relevant to a discussion of the repression. At the heart of this movement is a number of dedicated young priests who are disturbed both by the lack of religiosity in their parishes[10] and by a lack of social commitment on the part of the church hierarchy to the social problems of their parishioners. They feel that the Spanish church has become alienated from its flock because of its long and profound association with the nation's privileged classes. In their view, it is no longer sufficient to give charity to the poor; it is necessary to become recommitted to the people, in the broadest sense of the term. For the priests of the Young Catholic Workers, their commitment to the people touches every facet of human experience, of which politics is but one. These young men work tirelessly to solve all the problems their parishioners bring them, great and small, sacred and profane. Through the selflessness of their dedication, they have acquired a moral force that transcends religious boundaries. By setting good examples of personal and social comportment, they have steadily gained the respect of many people who are only nominally Catholic. They are exemplary people, clearly capable of teaching and helping others.

The political aspect of the work of the movement emphasizes recruiting the working class back into the religious fold by attempting to involve the workers in political action appropriate to their class. Class action and class consciousness are defined in political economy terms, with the priests identifying themselves as workers: "We are the proletariat, they [the large proprietors, the rich, the regime] are the bourgeoisie," was said to me at different times by different priests. Though at present, the ideology of the Young Catholic Workers is in flux, partly because of the difficulty of meshing Catholic doctrine with the themes of class struggle, this movement shows healthy signs of growth and activity.

The fact that such opposition has developed within the official power structure causes grave problems for the men in the municipal government. The Young Catholic Workers group has been subject to the same fines and harassment as have the associations, including the suspension of its newspaper, but the authorities must proceed cautiously because they are dealing with priests. Any precipitous move against the priests (such as their incarceration) would probably have repercussions among practicing Catholics, many of whom are very interested in the church reforms begun by Pope John XXIII, would cause considerable disgruntlement among less fervent Catholics who admire the priests for their good works, and might even provoke an inquiry on the part of the civil governor's office in Barcelona. Thus, up to a point, the local officials have to tolerate a growing political movement that ideologically has more universal appeal than parochial Catalan regionalism ever did.

Social aspects of governmental economic development efforts

Having discussed the economic impact of the government's efforts to modernize agriculture in the *comarca*, we now focus on the social organization and consequences of this intervention. In particular, we will discuss its effects on the local elite: large proprietors, small industrialists, and the high-status professionals–the local descendants of the nineteenth-century Catalan metropolitan bourgeoisie. Though they are the principal beneficiaries of the Franco regime, the government has exacted a stiff tariff in return for its beneficence. For as the regime aids the local elite in the course of economic modernization, it places this elite in a position of economic and political dependency on the regime. This new dependence upon the state goes a long way toward explaining the loss of dynamism among the local elite in economic endeavors.

How this dependence operates can be seen in the process of modernizing viniculture, a joint venture of the government and the local elite. A prime illustration is the earlier cited Agrarian Law of 1956, which provides government credits for the mechanization of properties, while imposing conditions to define the scope of action available to the proprietors. Machinery and credit are available only to those proprietors who will personally cultivate their land. The law is thus implicitly a frontal assault on the rentier basis of Catalan viticulture. In the past, the *rabassaire* was the principal victim of crop failures and declining wine prices; now the proprietor is asked to assume these risks. Nor is the proprietor allowed to put his newly acquired machinery immediately to use: He is prohibited by law from expelling the *rabassaires* from their plots and organizing the mechanization of his property. Each *rabassaire* must be paid a substantial indemnity for the land he cultivates. Considering these limitations on the initiative of the proprietors, it is hardly surprising that many choose to accept state credit and all its conditions, rather than risk their own capital to modernize their properties.

Another illustration of the local elite's dependence upon the regime is the *comarcal* viniculture cooperative. Clearly the cooperative represents a positive step toward improving the quality of common wines and therefore raising wine prices, but the politics of its founding are important in a social sense. It is noteworthy that twenty substantial proprietors petitioned the central government for 60 million pesetas in credits to construct the facilities, and were initially refused.[11] The credits were finally obtained as the result of a deal between a local large proprietor and a high official in Madrid that involved heavy financial commitment by the original interested parties. The local proprietor in question has served the government in various capacities; he was a politician of the Right prior to the war, in addition to his many activities as an agricultural entrepreneur. During his government service in Madrid, he had made many important political contacts. One of these contacts in the Ministry of Agriculture had sufficient power to quash the original veto, which had occurred at the provincial level of the bureaucracy, and to gain approval of the credits. However, allocation of credits was made contingent on certain crucial stipulations. Foremost among these was the proviso that the twenty founders of the cooperative would guarantee the state credits out of their own pockets. That is, the founding fathers were required to place personal funds totaling 60 million pesetas in a bank, to be held in escrow until the cooperative could repay the Ministry of Agriculture. In addition, they had to keep the cooperative's membership open to all cultivators, irrespective of holding size; instead of being a means of salvation only for large proprietors,[12] the cooperative was to provide staying power for the more progressive sharecroppers who would join a cooperative.[13]

At the risk of overgeneralizing from a single case, one can suggest that there is a pattern to the initial refusal of the credits and the final grant with its various stipulations. First, the request may well have been refused because an organized group of the local elite took the initiative in the matter, thereby placing the regime's provincial officials in a delicate position. After all, any shift in the local economy has implications for the outcome of the long-simmering land struggle in Catalonia between *rabassaire* and proprietor. This is the sort of political situation that the provincial administration is very cautious about. Second, navigating around the provincial veto was accomplished by a large proprietor who had contacts in the capital. His personal contacts and his staunch position as a "man of the Right" overcame his principal liability—his role as spokesman for an organized group of the Catalan bourgeoisie. The concessions exacted by the Ministry of Agriculture appear logical if viewed in the light of the 1956 Agrarian Law: They seek to make the liabilities of the local elite the same as the liabilities of the state. No closer financial symbiosis could be imagined than one in which the state requires its credits to be backed by the cash of those who receive such credits!

Apart from dynamic intervention in the local economy, with the local elite as a junior partner, the government has also focused its attention on the potential political consequences the resultant modernization might entail. This is particularly the case in light industry, where the *Organización Sindical* (state labor organization) takes over the role of adjudicating disputes between labor and management. Such disputes occur over management's hiring and firing policies, contribution of the employers to pension funds and health insurance, and the workers' right to payment for overtime. The guidelines of labor law, as we have seen earlier, have been fixed by the Ministry of Labor for the entire country. Implementing the labor laws is the province of the local *Organización Sindical*.

Such disputes occur with some frequency; although many owners seek to keep them within the factory, disputes over pensions frequently have to be settled by the *sindical*. This particular area of worker-management problems involved the *sindical* because of tax-evasion practices by factory owners. Pensions are paid on a percentage basis of the owners' declared earnings, upon which taxes are levied. To reduce taxes, owners report less than their true earnings—sometimes to the point that the reported earnings are so small that they prejudice the amount of the workers' pensions. This is the genesis of a dispute in which the *sindical* becomes involved.

The *sindical* is not a rubber stamp for the owners. In Vilafranca it seems to operate so well that neither the workers nor the owners like it; both are uncertain how disputes will be resolved. Whether these disputes are resolved in favor of one party or the other is secondary in importance to what is apparently the chief role of the *sindical:* to allow the government, rather than the owners, to deal with the political consequences of modernization in the industrial sector.

Despite the powerful constraints placed upon it by the government, the local elite is not totally without room for maneuver. Although the institutions of the state are powerful enough to coerce the local elite into economic and political dependence, the latter does its best to take advantage of the state in various small ways. Foremost among these is the manner in which members of the local elite can personally influence various kinds of state officials, particularly those involved in government agencies that supply technical aid and to a lesser extent those in the financial organizations of government. The payoffs for the local elite are small, but important. They involve slight bending of the law, getting an undue share of official technical advice, or receiving especially favorable consideration for credit petitions. The importance of this influence lies in the ability of certain members of the local elite to advance their own economic interests faster than other members of the elite who lack such contacts, and to do it with a minimum of strain. For example, if you are a rentier in viticulture who needs to modernize, and if you can make friends with various technical aid officials, you need not learn the intricacies of modern farming yourself in order to get the job done.

The method characteristically used by the local bourgeoisie to obtain influence with state officials involves a complex system of material inducement. State officials earn in general poor salaries – salaries that are frequently so small as to make it impossible for the recipients to live without some means of raising additional money. A suitably dignified means of augmenting one's official income is to accept a consultantship in some enterprise in the locale in which one is assigned. Because nearly all the relevant enterprises are owned by the local bourgeoisie, this class can offer the consultant-ships so necessary for the economic survival of the officials. Once this relationship is established, the bourgeoisie is able not only to get technical advice but often, with the aid of the grateful official, to make sure certain kinds of government regulations will be interpreted in an elastic manner.

The kind of material inducement represented by the consultant-ships should not be confused with graft, which consists of illicit payoffs and misappropriation of funds. Though graft is a well-known phenomenon in the Alto Panadés, it is still technically an aberration of the system and not synonymous with the system itself. The infinitesimal salaries of state officials make supplementary employment a structural requirement of their economic position; furthermore, it is perfectly legal. It could be argued that, far from occupying a "rational-bureaucratic" position, state officials actually occupy a variant of prebendal domain; that, their livelihood depends, not on salary, but on the generosity of their constituents, in this case, the local bourgeoisie. As popularly explained by officials and the bourgeoisie alike, this arrangement produces interesting payoffs for both parties and an equitable solution to their mutual problems.

Though the economic aspects of the relationships between government officials and the bourgeoisie are relatively straightforward, there are complicated social parameters to these arrangements which are problematical for both parties. Both have to make good assessments of the characters of their potential partners, particularly as regards loyalty and discretion, since each will come to know damaging facts about the other in the course of their transaction. The arena in which these assessments are made is, of course, the public bar, as discussed in Chapter 5. Given the complexities of the necessary interpersonal maneuvering in the bars, it is understandable that not all bourgeois can find loyal dependents, and not all officials can acquire all the consultantships they would like.

Three composite biographies are presented here to illustrate some common reactions of officials to their situation and of the bourgeoisie to the actions of these officials. Let us first consider the career of a successful official, Señor Tocaferro, who was until recently the director of a government agricultural monopoly. In his capacity as director of this state agency, Tocaferro earned an official salary of 1,000 pesetas a week; this is two-thirds the salary of an unskilled laborer in a local factory. He nonetheless managed to support his wife and eight children in a very comfortable fashion. Within a year after his arrival in the Alto Panadés, he had purchased an elegant and spacious apartment and a large automobile. He could be seen nearly every day in at least one of the fancy bars in Vilafranca, spending substantial sums of money to keep his friends well entertained. Apart from his effusive good treatment of his friends in the bars, he was blessed with a fine baritone voice and the ability to cook regional delicacies, two talents he used to build and maintain his vital contacts and friendships. Within three years, Tocaferro's position and personality had led him into consultantships in a number of wheat-flour mills and chicken-feed factories, each of which paid him much more than his monthly salary. Unfortunately, Señor Tocaferro was unable to content himself with his popularity and his consultantships. A government audit of his agency's books showed that much agricultural produce was mysteriously missing and disclosed a strategic malfunction in the scales being used to weigh incoming produce. Although graft taking could not be proved against him, the government meted out to him the worst punishment a Spanish bureaucrat can endure, short of imprisonment: He was transferred to a similar post in a very remote, poor mountainous district, where he presumably still languishes. His departure was considered by the local bourgeoisie to be a keen loss for Vilafranca.

A marked contrast to the departed Señor Tocaferro is provided by Señor Quixote. He has been for nearly thirty years a clerk in the same agency as Tocaferro, but unlike his former boss, has never solicited a peseta from anyone for any reason; he feels this would be a dishonest thing to do, a personal dishonor. He lives a life of reduced circumstances, surviving only because he has never married. He enjoys meeting his friends and acquaintances in the bars, but he steadfastly refuses to enter into any entangling alliances. Even to his friends, who have pleaded with him to take "what is rightfully his," he appears a hopeless romantic. To the bourgeoisie, his lack of utility, coupled with his romantic nature, make him something of a comic figure.

If the bourgeoisie is mildly exasperated by Señor Quixote's lack of utility, they are infuriated by Señor Recto, who is perhaps the most competent agrarian technician in the entire district. A product of one of the state government's technical schools, Recto has studied the agrarian problems of Spain profoundly from the technical standpoint. That is the trouble with Recto; he actually believes that modern technology is the answer to the problem and that all who farm must learn all about it. He does not perceive the social politics of modernization at all and shows not the slightest interest in bars and men's supper groups. Even worse, he actively encourages the sharecroppers to stay on their land and to learn the new techniques. Not only can Señor Recto not be hired, but his activities among the peasantry are rapidly making him anathema to the bourgeoisie.

These sketches of officials and the reaction to them on the part of the local bourgeoisie underline the subtler aspects of modernization and power in the Alto Panadés. Government programs offer possibilities for modernization primarily to those who are already in the strongest economic position in local society. Yet the realization of these possibilities depends on how well local officials and the bourgeoisie are able to relate to each other personally. The prospects for successful relationships are, in turn, influenced by complex social considerations, the most important of which is the tradition of strained relations between Catalans and the central government. In light of these difficulties, modernization in the Alto Panadés is proceeding more slowly than the dynamics of the economy seem to require.

7

Concluding remarks

The preceding chapters have traced the steady decline of Catalan regional cultural institutions and showed how this decline was precipitated by the Franco regime and the kind of modernization that it sponsored. The fate of the three institutions selected for study can be summarized as follows:

1. The *rabassa morta* sharecropping system, once the economic linchpin of the prosperous vinicultural economy of the late nineteenth and early twentieth centuries, is being eroded by continued stagnancy of the wine market and the gradual mechanization of the more substantial properties in the Alto Panadés. Consequently, the sharecropping class is rapidly becoming proletarianized, gaining employment either in service jobs or in jobs created by the influx of light industry into the district.

2. The *hereu-pubilla* marriage-inheritance system is becoming a thing of the past largely because the increasing concentration of property prevents most people from practicing it. In its place is arising the simple nuclear family, indicative of the weakening of kin ties in the area. The demise of the *hereu-pubilla* system corresponds with the demise of the small property ethic characteristic of rural Catalonia.

3. The cultural associations that harbored much of the political life and civic action of Catalonia have been repressed nearly to extinction by the Franco regime. Popular Catalanism cannot long remain a majority political stance, as the classes that originally supported it have either repudiated it (as in the case of the bourgeoisie) or are in an unsettled state (all the other classes). Increasingly, Catalanism is the exclusive domain of the surviving elements of the region's petite bourgeoisie, itself under considerable economic duress. With political life held in abeyance by the regime, bar culture has sprung up to replace the associations

as the most vital forum of public intercourse. In contrast to the collectivist spirit that characterized most of the associations, bar culture is concerned with individual economic and social advancement. The possibilities for such advancement are created by modernization.

At first glance, none of these social transformations seem extraordinary; they appear to be predictable outcomes of modernization. After all, in the face of modernization, peasants do become proletarianized, the importance of kin ties diminishes, individualist credos flourish at the expense of collectivist ones; in short, formerly distinct traditional cultures tend to converge on a single universal model of a wage-earning, largely industrial and urban, consuming society (Rostow 1961; Lipset 1968). Such transformations usually can be accounted for by the diffusion of technology and economies from the developed world to an underdeveloped country.

But Catalonia is in no way a traditional society; it is an advanced regional culture that generated an industrial revolution more than a century ago, and the fate of Catalonia is less the result of the workings of economics than of the exercise of power. Thus, this study has been informed with a theoretical matrix about the nature of modernization that ranks power higher than economics. Rather than assuming that Spain today is well on the road to national development, I have assumed that this government is leading the nation toward a dependent satellite position within the Western Capitalist bloc. Spain is not developing if we define "development" as "the process by which an underdeveloped region [or nation] attempts to acquire an autonomous and diversified industrial economy on its own terms" (Schneider et al., 1972:340).

But Spain, is certainly undergoing modernization, as discussed in Chapter 1. Spain is experiencing substantial foreign investment, which, in addition to its great tourist revenues, is sparking the growth of light industry and expansion of the service sectors of its economy. The capital generated by these activities is providing the basis for a consumer economy as well. All these developments depend heavily on the fostering of yet closer ties to the economies of the developed nations of the West. This growing matrix of dependency makes the study of Catalan culture pertinent to any discussion of the course of economic growth and social change in the underdeveloped world. Catalan culture underwent a gradual evolution toward a bourgeois society over many centuries, emerging in the 1800s as capable of challenging the archaic elites that had misruled Spain for so long. That it took the force of German arms and political abstention on the part of other developed powers (France, Britain, England, and the United States) ultimately to defeat, not the Catalan bourgeoisie, but the society it had created, is an interesting testimony to the attitude of the great powers toward developmentally inclined regions in the third world.

The demise of rural Catalan culture cannot be discussed only in terms of the rise and fall of the Catalan bourgeoisie; even though that class sparked the region's drive toward Catalan preeminence within Spain in the last century, it did not do so as individuals alienated from the stultifying matrix of a traditional agrarian society, but as an elite standing at the apex of a society that was eminently commercial in nature. The Catalan bourgeois was not the alienated bourgeois discussed by Rostow (1961) or the nonconformist of Lipset (1968). He was rather both creation and creator of his own society, an individual fully integrated in a society that had come to relish the ideals of productivity and property. The defeat and eclipse of the bourgeoisie occurred at the hands of the southern and central Spanish elites, which represented, not feudalism but *dependent capitalism,* of which the Franco regime is a modern expression (Schneider et al. 1972:340–3).

The collapse of rural Catalan culture can partly be explained by the political defeat of the Catalan bourgeoisie by these elites and by the popular classes in Catalonia. As explained in Chapter 2, the cultural institutions studied in this work were largely shaped by the bourgeoisie in the course of its own lengthy evolution. Not only did these institutions shape the social and economic life of most rural Catalans, but their symbolic overlays provided an ideological basis for the bourgeois populism of the late nineteenth and early twentieth centuries. Both the institutions and the populism were representative of the Catalan bourgeoisie in its developmental phase, the period when it sought to usher in an industrial revolution. The political defeat of the Catalan bourgeoisie involves a repudiation of the very culture it had labored so long to create.

Several anthropologists have advanced the following argument about the fate of regionalism in the western Mediterranean. Regionalism cannot exist without a regional elite that enjoys some autonomy from the central government and some support from the popular classes in its own domain. Critical to the maintenance of regional power domains by regional elites is the creation of social organization, both formal and informal, based on regional cultural ideology. When the power of the regional elites is usurped by central governments (as has been increasingly the case in the western Mediterranean since the 1930s), regionalism begins to disintegrate. Symptomatic of this disintegration are (1) the dramatic and sudden irrelevance of regional formal social organization, (2) the restricted scope and functions of informal social organization, and (3) a reorganization of cultural ideology by the now-dependent elite, which negates regionalism and frequently substitutes an exaltation of individualism, coupled with a strong stress on law and order (Schneider et al. 1972:345–50).

All these symptoms are well developed in the Alto Panadés. Much of this study is devoted to tracing the demise of the formal cultural institutions, but the last two symptoms require some amplification. The emergent bar culture is the major milieu of their expression. The Catalan bourgeois has been reduced by the central government to the position of a wealthy individual fishing for sometimes recalcitrant clients in the fancy bars of Vilafranca. He is offered the opportunity to gain more wealth through modernization, but he must modernize on the government's terms, not his own. To receive economic benefits from the government, he must repudiate *Catalanism,* the traditional rallying point for all Catalans, and risk alienating other Catalans who still adhere to these sentiments. In this context of powerlessness and hostility "barroom democracy" has emerged.

Bar culture is a negation of political ideology and social vision; it substitutes the exaltation of individual success for the traditional Catalan social consciousness. Its idiom obscures the fundamental social problems of the Alto Panadés, which touched off a revolution only two generations ago. It suppresses social class differences between individuals and eliminates consideration of the social outcomes of modernization that its participants seek to usher in. This is replaced by an emphasis on hedonism, typified by ritual gluttony. The need to consume things embraces other areas besides food and drink; Scotch whisky has become the prestige drink (replacing local wines) at the bars; the cult of the automobile is growing; an addiction to American movies and TV is developing. The picture is completed by fascination with tourist life on the nearby Mediterranean coast, including a keen interest in the sexual mores of bikini-clad girls from permissive northern countries. Modernization clearly affects more than social and economic life; it appears to have glandular side effects as well.

Superficially, the coalitions forged in Vilafranca's bars seem to be characteristically Mediterranean, particularly in their structural dimensions: They are informally arranged, have a developed ideology of interpersonal relationships based on personal prestige, and involve a host of patron-client ties. Yet compared with other well-known Mediterranean vertical coalitions, such as the Mafia (see P. Schneider 1969; J. Schneider 1969; Blok 1972), the coalitions in the Alto Panadés are quite restricted in scope and function. Whereas in Sicily, Mafia ties fan out throughout the economy and political structure of the island, all real power of the Catalan bourgeoisie has been preempted by the state. As a result, these men can only enter into small-scale, local (not even regional) coalitions with the express goal of modernizing their viticultural estates or setting up mainly service industries. Thus no real power can be mobilized through informal coalition formation; it would be ludicrous to imagine the members of even the largest coalition leaping to their feet after an enormous dinner and challenging the power of the central government.

In fine, the Catalan bourgeoisie appears to have made the transition from a *developmental* to a *dependence* elite. Its loss of autonomy and initiative under the Franco regime is clear; it is now simply one elite among many others in Spain, all clearly subordinate to the state, in its turn increasingly reliant upon the developed nations of the Western Capitalist bloc. Like the emergent bourgeoisie in many underdeveloped nations, it has become an elite that has settled for money when power eluded it.[1] The only thing this bourgeoisie has managed to do in the transition is maintain what properties it already had and, with the aid of the state, augment them in some cases. Perhaps the economic strength of the Catalan bourgeoisie will ultimately be sorely tested by the inroads of foreign capital investment now evident even in the Alto Panadés.

If the Catalan bourgeoisie has become progressively denatured by the process of modernization and dependency, the popular classes are undergoing an even more profound transformation. Both their means of livelihood and the quality of their aspirations are being changed rapidly. With the increasing concentration and rising costs of property, the bourgeois ethic of property acquisition is becoming increasingly irrelevant to the facts of economic life in rural Catalonia. As they become increasingly dependent upon wages, their situation is becoming increasingly proletarianized. But wage differentials and the creation of new kinds of socioeconomic opportunities will offer them a measure of social mobility. Out of modernization one kind of middle class will likely arise, but one that can only consume, not one that can have a serious impact on the politcal life of the region and the nation. Dependent on the vagaries of a somewhat artificial economy, it will likely be analogous to the unstable Latin American classes described by Nun (1967).

Apart from gross economic and political aspects of their position in the process of modernization, the popular classes are also undergoing a cultural transformation. The kind of life style and mobility offered encourage, even force, them to embrace a consumer culture with largely foreign status components. It is a culture that places a greater premium on a watch, a gabardine coat, and a TV set than on anything traditionally valued in the regional culture, including the desire to be an autonomous united people. The new consumer culture is based on a distorted notion of what life is like in the developed countries derived from observation of the carryings-on of tourists. To embrace this imagery wholeheartedly is to search for will-o'-the-wisp. Pursuit of the consumer culture also involves a noticeable amount of social deracination, since it negates the cultural supports learned in childhood. This deracination, as much as the high economic stakes involved, is likely the cause of the deadening, persistent nervous tension of the emergent bar culture.

APPENDIX

Field procedures

Anthropological research on the problems of national development and power is still new, but the course of history is drawing us relentlessly to study them. I offer the following account of my field procedures in the hope that those doing fieldwork on these problems will at least be spared my errors. Perhaps they will find some of the techniques discussed here useful to their own research. This account is not only for anthropologists; it is for anyone interested in the way information for this study was collected in the field.

No effort is made here to give an exhaustive account of all the techniques used in this study. Many are common and merit only a small mention: Like every anthropologist, I counted heavily on informants, participant observation, and open-ended interviews for much of my information. I also kept a field journal, writing down each day's events as I lived them and periodically reviewing the journal in search of insights or leads that had initially eluded me. Additionally, I recorded many genealogies and traced many networks of people. That I did these things is less interesting than the context of the research strategies they related to. No technique is worth discussing or using unless it relates to some coherent body of theory – an interpretive scheme. I originally designed this study in line with that body of theory known generally as political economy, modified by some explicitly anthropological theories relating to the functions of informal coalitions in complex societies (e.g., Leeds 1964; Wolf and Hansen, 1967). After the interplay of field data and my intellectual sensibilities had wrecked my original model, I started working on a better one in conjunction with Peter and Jane Schneider, who were having similar difficulties with their Sicilian research. Jointly we developed the conceptual scheme set forth in Chapter 1 of this book and in Schneider et al., 1972. The techniques discussed below relate to that model and no other (except, of course, by extrapolation).

This exposition is limited by time and space to a consideration of two major research questions and some of their ramifications. First, given an interest in developmental questions, what is the appropriate *unit of study:* a community, a class, several classes, a region? Second, what is the relationship between *formal* and *informal* social organizations and what are their respective roles in the developmental process? In other words, what are the institutional arrangements of the society (social classes, bureaucracy, etc.) and how do they relate to the interpersonal coalitions based on friendship and clientage so familiar to students of Mediterranean societies? Let us examine each of these intimately related problems briefly.

The region as unit of study: how I wound up in the Alto Panadés

The nature of the study dictated that I select a place that was a microcosm of all of rural Catalonian society. That ruled out the traditional anthropological approach of studying a single unit of human habitation, such as a community or a town. If I contented myself with a rural community, I could look only at *rabassaires,* a handful of petit bourgeois storekeepers, and maybe five large landholders. If I chose to locate in Vilafranca, I could study only the commercial relationships within the town and the goings-on in the bars. I would miss dealing with the *rabassaires* and fail to observe crucial aspects of agrarian production.

For these reasons, I decided to study a juridical district, since it had both towns and rural villages, and therefore a good representation of all the social classes, as well as an integrated economic structure that could be observed at first hand. Additionally, a juridical district, as an administrative unit of the government, contains at least one center where the organs of government are concentrated (in this case, Vilafranca). Initially, I had hoped to pick a district closer to Barcelona, where the impact of metropolitan expansion could be easily examined. The one I chose from an outdated geographical account of Catalan rural districts had, however, become a working-class suburb of the city. Disconsolate at my ignorance, I sought the advice of a Catalan artist about where to locate. A native of the Panadés, he assured me it was the most beautiful of all the rural *comarcas* and badly in need of anthropological inquiry. Moreover, he warned me, most rural Catalonians were beasts, while those of the Panadés were "super-civilized."

Convinced by the intellectual force of his argument, I quickly found my way to the Alto Panadés, where I began to face the real problems of selecting a unit of study. I was only one person among 45,000 Catalans, who were spread out among twenty-three villages and two towns. Clearly it would be impossible to shake all their hands in the course of fieldwork, let alone participant observe them or take their genealogies. I had to select a sample of local people that would represent the Alto Panadés, which in turn represented rural Catalonia.

As I was concerned with problems of development, placed in a political economy context, I decided to follow the chains of human relationships that grew out of the productive process. I placed particular emphasis on vini- and viticulture, since the Alto Panadés was famous for its wine, but various factories were studied as well. I tried to observe all the steps of productivity, the people involved, and the quality of their relationships. As soon as I began to do this, I realized that there were at least fifty people directly involved in the process of getting grapes out of the ground, into the bottle, and sold to the public. I realized that if I could study about ten of these chains of people exhaustively, I would have a good idea of the various ways in which this could be done, and a sample of over 500 people as well. I reasoned that I would get a good idea of the range of productive behavior and at the same time achieve a measure of mathematical respectability for my study.

The structure of the economy allowed me to begin with the haute bourgeoisie, since it was the linchpin of the economy. Apart from its historical significance, this class controlled the larger estates, much of the real estate, and many of the local factories. Alone, these people would make a good study, but my own research was geared to dealing first with them and then following their connections both to the working class, the *rabassaires*, and the petite bourgeoisie (particularly in service enterprises), and to government officials and major capitalists operating outside of the district.

This concentration on the haute bourgeoisie immediately simplified my problem; there were only 250 such families in the entire district. Thus the core of my fieldwork effort was tracing in great detail the web of social relationships surrounding these few individuals. This process led me through villages and estate houses, tourist spas and factories, and onto the floor of the Barcelona stock exchange, and it focused the study by delineating the sample. When one considers the advantages of studying elites – their small number, their position of power, their social coherence, their intricate webs of intermarriage – one is amazed that elites are not studied more often and in greater detail.

This selection also helped me in another way; it called attention to the proliferation of informal coalitions that abound in the Alto Panadés and that are so influential in shaping the course of modernization in the district. My original research design stressed the more formal aspects of the role of power in modernization, but I quickly realized that much more than bureaucracy and contractual obligation were needed to make things work in the Alto Panadés. Following these chains of productive resources brought me right into the public bars of Vilafranca, where I could observe the fluid character of modernization in the district. Thus, by virtue of a fairly commonsensical approach to the problem of the unit of study, I laid out the basic lines of inquiry within the first three months of research. The next task was to set up a sharper matrix for inquiry into the more formal aspects of society.

Examination of formal institutions: classes and power

To develop a picture of the institutional matrix of local society and to check on the representativeness of my selection of people, I had to compile a body of statistical information on the workings of the economy, demography, the marriage system, and so forth. In this task I was greatly aided by various local people who were studying these things or keeping records of them in some official capacity. Just prior to my coming to the Alto Panadés, many aspects of the economy (land tenure, levels of mechanization, crop yields, agricultural practices, etc.) and demography (population curves of all villages and towns by decade for the past century) had been extensively studied under the aegis of the state labor organization. Thus, by luck I was able to get manuscript copies of the various reports cited in the text and was saved the arduous task of collecting this information myself. Since the men who had carried out the various studies were all in Vilafranca, I was able to discuss their work with them and form a high opinion (in most cases) of its worth.

Vilafranca, as head of the juridical district, also proved a rich source of records, so rich that I could not use them all as much as I would have liked. For example, the Enology Station kept records on all facets of wine production and was staffed by people with insight into the social history of agriculture. The local notary's office was a gold mine of statistics on *hereu-pubilla* transactions. Excellent records of property transactions (including many involving tax frauds) were contained in the property registry. Marriages could be traced from the parish office of the basilica. Historical documents on the Panadés from the ninth century onward were available in the local museum, although not yet catalogued well enough to be of great value.

Once I had built up my body of statistical information and made sufficient personal contacts, I felt ready to begin interviewing members of the haute bourgeoisie and their dependents. Accordingly, I drew up an open-ended questionnaire, designed to provide data on the following topics: size of property holding, style of management, attitudes toward government policies affecting agriculture, familial biography (including genealogies), and relations toward other social classes (particularly employees and sharecroppers). Questions were left open-ended to encourage a variety of responses and to allow conversational expansiveness on the part of the interviewee. I conducted some fifty interviews with members of the bourgeoisie which ranged in length from about two hours to three entire days.

Initially, the interviewing process went very slowly because I was overly polite and solicitous about seeking interviews with people I hardly knew. I made the error of being too formal, which made these people suspicious of me. My mistake was brought home to me forcefully by one of the few nobles remaining in the Alto Panadés, whom I had interviewed by chance. He explained in no uncertain terms that I was behaving like a servant or client to these individuals when my own wealth, looks, and education meant that I was superior to them. Therefore, he said, I should command them to give me interviews. He proceeded to accompany me to more than twenty bourgeois landholders, and ordered them to give me what I wanted, on the spot, including details of business scandals, etc. All complied, some with obeisance toward the count, and all with both deference and expansiveness toward me. The count checked all their answers to see if they were concealing vital information. Astonished and embarrassed as I was, the count had a point: After these twenty interviews, I was swamped by volunteers. It had suddenly become fashionable to be interviewed by *el distinguido antropólogo norteamericano*. Starting with these bourgeois landholders, I administered the same interviews to representatives of other social classes. During the course of several months, I managed to interview more than 150 different people, distributed roughly equally among the petite bourgeoisie, the working class, and the *rabassaires*. Thus between collecting the statistical information and conducting the interviews, I felt I was in a good position to understand much about the nature of class relationships in the Alto Panadés. I had not only the requisite information on property structure and commerce, but also a rich collection of the perceptions of the classes of themselves and of each other. I had also learned an important personal lesson: The informal way is the only way to work in the Mediterranean.

Despite my good fortune in having ready access to statistical material and interviewees, one very knotty problem perplexed me during my work. The "chains of productive relations" technique I was pursuing would lead me inexorably to government officials, who, because of the repression, were anathema to many people in the popular classes. To consort with them would have seriously compromised my efforts to follow my chains downward. Every anthropologist is thought to be a spy anyway, and to be perceived as a spy for the Franco government would have been ruinous to my work, apart from offending my sensibilities. I therefore chose not to spend much time associating with officials, even though I believe many of them would have made an honest and significant contribution to the study. This choice meant that much of the study of power had to be done by indirection. In retrospect, I believe I may have been overcautious in avoiding these officials and possibly could have studied their actions directly toward the end of the fieldwork, when I was already an established personality in Vilafranca.

Study of informal social organization: how to survive and do research while eating and drinking copiously

Any study of power has to come to grips with the problem of finding out how to research informal social organization, since many crucial payoffs are realized outside the official structure. In addition to studying the institutional arrangements of power, it is necessary and useful to study informal networks of people along the lines proposed by Barnes (1968) and Barth (1966). The techniques of network analysis are extremely simple; they involve the tracing out of who is connected with whom and in what way. Every society is full of networks, but only a few networks out of many are relevant to a study of power. Again, prior to undertaking network analysis, it is crucial to place one's networks in some analytical context – in this case, power.

No one even remotely familiar with the literature on the western Mediterranean would underestimate the role of the informal coalition in the region's political life. In this part of the world, power has long been fragmented into different domains. Much of political life has been dominated by personalist political structures that come to embrace everyone in the population, minimally through patron-clientage and instrumental friendships. In spite of the expansion of state power, so evident in the area from the 1930s onward, small-scale coalitions continue to function, although with reduced scope of power. These coalitions should not be confused with "traditional" or "transitional" organizations because they organize many crucial modern economic functions. In the Panadés, the process of modernization is not understandable without them.

Finding the proper networks to analyze in the field was not simply a matter of operationalizing my theoretical constructs, but also a question of good luck. The man who convinced me to go to the Alto Panadés happened to have an uncanny sense about whom I should meet to prosecute my study and knew precisely where to find them. He brought me to one of the fancy bars immediately and sent word around town that he was visiting Vilafranca with a foreign anthropologist in tow. Within half an hour, about a dozen men arrived at the bar, and over champagne, we discussed briefly some aspects of my work. It turned out that these men represented a crucial cross section of "who was who" in the area – politically, socially, and economically. These men opened all doors for me, particularly in terms of getting more and more useful contacts. Throughout my field stay, they continually made every effort to make sure I was getting the kind of information I needed for the study. Often they were able to suggest things I had not even thought of doing.

All of them insisted that when I did not have interviews or was not investigating local archives, I should repair to one of the bars and wait for something to happen. This turned out to be splendid advice for the times I was at loose ends. I met an enormous variety of people at the bar, and it was an ideal place to begin tracing networks because the coalitions described in Chapter 5 were being formed right before my eyes. I suspect that bars would be a good place for field inquiry almost anywhere in Spain. The only real operational problem posed is endurance. The canons of hospitality require one to eat and drink heavily, and frequently to stay out late at night. As a result of tracing networks in the bars, I gained about thirty pounds in the field.

The most difficult intellectual part of the analysis of the coalitions is coming to grips with the nature of the prestige competition that results in the ranking of members in the coalitions. It is easy to see that there are ranking principles at play, but they are wrapped in a complicated cultural code. Cracking this code is difficult for the participants themselves: No one knows the whole of it, and most know only enough to play the prestige game. However well trained a foreign anthropologist may be, what is difficult to the cultural insider is almost unfathomable to the outsider. Yet it is precisely a knowledge of the code that leads to an understanding of the dynamics of these coalitions.

In order to tackle this problem, I spent the entire summer of 1969 applying Silverman's (1966) method of studying prestige-deference ethnographically. Her method stresses that the code must be elicited from local people, who are charged with the task of ranking specific individuals, without interference from the social scientist. Any number of informants are given a list of people (my own list contained 100 names, 25 drawn from each social class), and asked to rank them according to the prestige they enjoy. When the ranking process is completed, they are asked to explain their criteria, which are carefully noted down by the anthropologist as a partial vocabulary of the code. I asked each of the informants to give me a brief description of every individual on the list, in a fairly successful attempt to catch the repetitive elements in the evaluations. I then made up a hierarchy of evaluative statements based on the frequencies of such thematic responses and tried to explain the functions of what I discerned to be the local prestige-deference system. Finally I tested the ranking system by having other people rank the list by means of a card sort (without descriptions). Their concurrence with the rankings of the informants confirmed the accuracy of the latter's evaluation. Though I could not fathom all the nuances of the prestige system, I believe I got enough of them to understand the rudiments of coalition formation in the Alto Panadés.

Looking back at the research now that several years have passed, I believe many things could have been done somewhat differently, although the basic approach still seems correct. One thing that stands out in my mind is that this kind of study could best have been done by several people, working in conjunction, rather than by a single person. First, there was more information available than it was physically possible for me to collect. Second, because I benefited from visits by people with different perspectives from my own, I feel that working more extensively with people of different disciplines (history, political science, etc.) would have been rewarding. Finally, working in conjunction with others would probably have given a greater time dimension for the observations made in the field, since the work could have been spread out over more time. Despite all the ego problems this could involve, I believe the complexities of this kind of research can be handled better by a team than by an individual.

NOTES

Chapter 1. A government, a region, and the Alto Panadés

1 A juridical district is a political unit roughly equivalent to a county under the present Spanish administration.

2 This concept of modernization has little to do with the way the term is generally used in the literature to describe the path of underdeveloped countries toward economic growth. Its proponents do not believe that the process of modernization will lead underdeveloped countries through the same evolutionary trajectory followed by European countries during the Industrial Revolution (Rostow 1961) or that even if the same path is not followed because of a "late development effect," all underdeveloped countries will ultimately become urban industrial nations (Moore 1966; Bendix 1967; Dore 1969).

3 A useful and intricate analysis of the present Spanish economy is provided by Ramón Tamames (1965, 1970).

4 Tourism in places like Spain, Yugoslavia, and Mexico deserves special study, not merely because of its increasing importance in the economies of many underdeveloped nations, but also because of its cultural impact on the local people.

5 The conservative cast of the cabinet ministers is also reflected in their social profiles. Some 72 percent of the cabinet ministers are associated with the professions of the traditional wealthy in Spain. According to Linz (1962:330, 333–4), 42 percent were lawyers, 25 percent academics, and 4 percent in the health professions.

6 A few farmers whose holdings are large enough to permit it make contacts with the handful of shepherds who still traverse the Alto Panadés. These contracts provide food and lodging for the itinerant herds and their guides, in exchange for the manure the sheep leave in their corrals.

7 Built into one face of this mountain is the Abbey of Montserrat, a ninth-century monastery that attracts numerous pilgrims each year from all Catalan regions as well as from Navarre.

8 The erection of human towers (*els castellers* or *els Xiquets*) is the quintessential Catalan sport, the regional equivalent of bullfights in pretourist Andalusia. Like most Catalan popular activities, *els xiquets* involves mass participation and is consequently a great social leveler. Each major town in Catalonia has at least one team of *castellers*, consisting of roughly two dozen men and boys. The teams compete with each other during major festivals in making human towers. Crowd participation comes in the forms of supporting the base of these towers (i.e., the strongest and most corpulent men) and cushioning the men's falls when the towers collapse (a frequent occurrence). It is tempting to suggest that this sport is a metaphor for Catalan society's collective image, stressing that all Catalans rise and fall together.

9 By culture-free, I mean that only the means of production are considered, not the symbolic trappings that surround what we call "culture." Thus, a worker at a lathe in a factory in Vilafranca is the same as a person similarly employed in the United States, regardless of the fact that one is Spanish and the other is American (Stavenhagen 1967).

Chapter 2. Growth of modern Catalonian regionalism

1 Olivares, the favorite and principal minister of Philip IV, made valiant attempts both to rationalize and to increase the power of the monarchy at the expense of the regions of the realm. These policies caused repeated revolts in the regions, the most serious of which were the rebellions of the Portuguese and the Catalans (Elliott 1963a).

2 The "six evil uses" are summarized by Merriman (1936:1:478) from the original study of Hinojosa (1918:233–44, 367) as follows (I omit the *remenca*, as it is discussed in the text): "The second was the *intestia* or the right of the lord to a share – one-third or even one-half of the goods of a peasant who died intestate. The third, the *exorquia*, gave the lord the privilege of appropriating a portion of the property of a serf who died without issue. The fourth, the *cugucia*, adjudged to him the whole or part of the property of any peasant's wife guilty of adultery. The fifth, the *arsina*, compelled the peasant to pay the lord an indemnity if the whole or part of his farm should be burned. Lastly, the *firma de spoli* permitted the lord to exact a contribution from a serf who desired to pledge the proceeds of his farm to the woman he proposed to wed, pending the payment of her dowry and the performance of the marriage ceremony."

3 According to Giralt i Raventós (1966:17), the white and blond varieties of Panadés wheat were sufficiently delicate to be the favorite foods of the higher clergy of Barcelona during this period.

4 The Golden Century is a misnomer. This literary period starts with de Rojas's *La Celestina*, published in 1499, and extends through the reign of Philip III and the writings of Quevedo (1580–1645), particularly *Los Sueños (The Dreams)*.

5 The "administrator" of the original *boutique*, in Alegre's case Fransech Pujet, was also free to follow the same course. By 1758, Pujet had passed out of the category of *boutique* administrator and was one of the founders of the *Corps de Comerce* (Vilar 1962:III:384).

6 Shipbuilding was an associational enterprise of the financial associates, the *barca*, and the crews and equipment personnel. At first, the boats built were small, as their trips were limited to short-distance coastal trade. Increasing commercialization, however, intensified this trade and industry. A single boat, for instance, was able to repay its cost in four years, assure an interest of 5 percent to its shareholders for ten years, and ensure the livelihood of a small group of artisans who also had participated on a joint stock basis (Vilar 1962:III:202).

7 Vilar (1962:II:324) writes that a characteristic reaction of the French colonists in Louisiana annexed to the Spanish Empire after the Treaty of Paris was the fear that they would have imposed on them, instead of Bordeaux wines, "those poisonous Catalan wines." Vilar suggests that this was not a connoisseur's disgust, but the reaction of French merchants to the extension of the Spanish monopoly.

8 When a deputy to the Cortes complained to the minister, José Echegaray, in 1874, saying, "all we have left to hand over is the air we breathe," that philosopher, man of letters, and politician answered him disdainfully: "That is a concern unworthy of the times we live in" (Vicens Vives 1969:658).

9 The Bank of Spain was established in 1868; until then credit was largely ceded by individuals. Market conditions in the interior of Spain, the largest Catalan market, were chronically unstable throughout the nineteenth century (Vicens Vives 1961:128–9).

10 Between 1800 and 1900, the population of Barcelona increased more than six times over its population in 1800, from 85,000 to 533,000, as a consequence of its industrial growth (Vicens Vives 1961:41).

11 Tariff limits were maintained on yarn whose thread count was below twenty, which was what was used in Catalonian factories (Vicens Vives 1969:708).

12 These titles were known as *títulos pontíficos* (papal titles), and though it is popularly believed in the Alto Panadés that they were dispensed only to rich people who had to pay

for them, they were in fact granted by the Spanish crown at the behest of the nobility. In the Alto Panadés today, there is not a single noble of lineage remaining, though there are four large landholders who have *títulos pontíficos* granted their families during the nineteenth century.

13 Carlism was a clerical and monarchical movement involving peasants and priests who wished to place Don Carlos, brother of Ferdinand VII (and later his descendants), upon the Spanish throne. Although the movement consistently backed the restoration of absolute monarchy, its strongest goal was the devolution of local liberties to all Spanish regions (Brenan 1962:28, 203–14).

14 These were the National Property Act of 1836 and the Madoz Law of 1855.

15 Two other Carlist wars succeeded that of 1833–40, one beginning in 1845 and lasting four years, and the final war taking place from 1872 to 1876. After the first war, Carlism was effectively broken as a serious political force. The second and third Carlist wars were limited in scope and intensity in comparison with the war of 1833–40. See Mas i Perera 1932:76–8 for the path of the Carlist wars in the Alto Panadés.

16 As will be discussed in Chapter 3, the emerging bourgeoisie at the end of the eighteenth century had been most eager to end the *rabassa morta* contract and shorten the time of the lease, regardless of the state of the vines on the land, to take advantage of rising land prices and lease prices (Vilar 1962:II:504–15). The Madrid Cortes had sided with the *rabassaires* during the ensuing conflict of the 1790s, but had left the establishment of new contracts to the discretion of the landowners. In late-eighteenth-century conditions the establishment of new long-term contracts was unlikely. The reactivation of the contract in the nineteenth century can be understood only within the context of the bourgeoisie's search for diversification of its holdings and for stability to counteract the vagaries of the Spanish market and industrial economy.

17 In 1869 this body was reorganized into the Employers' Association, which became heavily involved in national electoral politics (Brenan 1962:29).

18 Shortly after the Franco uprising in July 1936 all the bourgeoisie crossed over to the insurgents' territory (Garcia Venero 1953:136).

Chapter 3. Political economy of land tenure in the Alto Panadés

1 *Aparcería* is a sharecropping contract that lasts for one year only. This contract is now the prevalent juridical instrument regulating sharecropping in the Alto Panadés and has since 1939 largely replaced the *rabassa morta* contract.

2 In 1907, French vintners of the champagne district sued Catalan vintners over the latter's appropriation of the name "champagne" for their product. The French vintners won their case, so Spanish champagne has since been sold under the name *vino espumoso* (sparkling wine).

3 The denaturing of the original *rabassa morta* contract began in the 1780s, when rising land values made landlords prefer shorter leases. See Giralt i Raventós (1964) for a full history of the contract.

4 The Catalan word *colgats* literally refers to the suckers on the grapevine, but local usage denotes the practice described in the text.

5 During the late eighteenth-century *rabassa* conflict, this practice was forbidden for a time, but losses to the landlords' shares were so great that the law forbidding *colgats* was ignored, though the contract's limit was maintained at fifty years (Vilar 1962:II:504–15; Giralt i Raventós 1964:57–8).

6 Viticulture cooperativism in Catalonia began in the 1890s in the neighboring Campo de Tarragona. The Bajo Panadés, the next juridical district south of the Alto Panadés, has numerous village viticulture cooperatives. For the history of early cooperatives in Catalonia, see Campllonch (1917).

7 Mas i Perera (1932:80) cites one example of a terrorist organization called the Black Hand, which operated in one village and was reputedly linked to anarchists in Barcelona. However, there is no report that this organization actually terrorized anyone. As it does not appear in any later literature, one can assume it was short-lived.

8 In general, such schools were lay schools that tried to break the monopoly of the church on the education of children.

9 Cooperatives in Campo de Tarragona occasionally led to the formation of sharecropper communes philosophically committed to anarchism. One such case was that of Conca de Barberá.

10 The earliest viticulture cooperative in Catalonia was Conca de Barberá (Campo de Tarragona), founded in 1894 by the *rabassaires* of that remote village (Campllonch 1917:40).

11 Both *rabassaires* and large proprietors agree on this point when discussing events during the civil war.

12 The tractor is the basic instrument of mechanization in the vineyards; separate machines are attached to the tractor to perform the various tasks necessary to cultivate a vineyard. Operations that can be mechanized at present are plowing, weeding, and application of chemical treatments to the vineyards. Harvesting and pruning of dead suckers still have to be done manually, and these tasks are performed in only three weeks of the year. Because machinery is so expensive, it is usually bought in stages, as the owner can afford it, beginning with the tractor (Giró 1966:5).

13 This figure was cited to me by various land speculators and large proprietors during my interviews.

14 Forty-six out of fifty-one large proprietors stated during interviews that they wished to acquire more land, but could not compete with metropolitan and foreign interests seeking land for tourist installations or light industry.

15 Terms and conditions of the Agrarian Credit Law of 1954 are set forth in *Decreto 16 de Junio de 1954 (Ministerio de Agricultura)* Boletín Oficial 7 de Julio, *Crédito Agrícola, Texto Refundido de sus Leyes Reguladores.*

16 Most sons of large proprietors, according to the sample I interviewed, studied some branch of commerce or law, if they studied at all past the age of fourteen. Until this generation, agriculture was for the *rabassaire,* not for the gentlemen.

17 Giró (1966:6), using the cost-analysis method, argues that machinery cuts production costs in vineyard. However, his computation includes a hypothesized wage for the *rabassaire,* which is not paid. Without this stipulated wage, sharecropping is cheaper.

18 This information was provided independently by various of the prime movers in the cooperative movement.

19 Villages in the valley are no doubt losing their sharecroppers as well, but demographic loss does not show up in the population reports because of replacement by industrial workers moving to this area.

20 No statistics are kept on decline in number of lawsuits. However, all lawyers who have handled such cases in the past agree that since 1960 the number of such suits has declined radically and that at present virtually none are being filed.

21 In 1966, the minimum daily wage in Spain was 60 pesetas ($1). The average daily wage in the Alto Panadés for semiskilled labor was between 180 and 240 pesetas.

Chapter 4. Erosion of the small property ethic

1 A "marriage-succession system" is used by Arensberg and Kimball (1940) to describe one integrated set of social relationships that governs land tenure, family form and roles, and property succession.

2 The juridical essentials of the *hereu-pubilla* inheritance system and the related *capitols matrimonials* are discussed in Maspons i Anglasells (1935).

3 Much of this information came from intimate friends who were willing to discuss these affairs with me. Good sources of information were the records of individual lawyers who handled cases relating to inheritance conflicts and court records of the jurdical district. One source of information on *capitols* was the parish offices of the village priests, who on occasion serve the function of notary public in drawing up the *capitols*.

4 Greater fortunes can, of course, be had in the industrial sector of Barcelona, where the firms are much bigger than in the Alto Panadés. The rural contingent of the haute bourgeoisie is generally not as well off as the urban one, although there is considerable overlap between the two.

5 It is interesting to note that five of the interviewees stressed that their formal training and breeding were inspired by English models of comportment, particularly the ideological stress of the English on formality in business negotiations.

6 Fifty interviews from the wealthy bourgeoisie means that I have a sample of 100 heirs, 50 in the present generation and 50 for the future.

7 Younger daughters are seldom considered appropriate candidates for any kind of education.

8 Usually all children, regardless of social class, attend either religious or public schools until the age of fourteen, at which time they receive their high school diplomas. The vast majority of children then begin apprenticeships in the professions they will pursue as adults.

9 This is not the only way business partnerships are formed in the district. Equally many are made between friends.

10 "Castilians" here refers not only to natives of that region, but to all those Spaniards who speak Castilian as their native tongue. To the Catalans, they are all "foreigners."

11 A youth I interviewed was one of the more famous examples of a stray bullet. He dissipated a $300,000 inheritance in land to stake himself to skiing trips in Switzerland, adventures with drugs on the coast, and romantic ventures in the Nordic countries – all before the age of twenty-one.

12 A sum of $285 represents only a fraction of the annual earnings of a sharecropper, which usually total in excess of $1,000. Yet in spite of the small amounts contested for, the section of the court dealing with these cases does much more business than the regular court does in suits over $285.

13 In Spain records of marriages are entered in the parish in which a person was born, not the one where he lives (or even in the church where he is actually married) at the time of his marriage. The records in the Vilafranca parishes do not reflect the rapid growth of the town in the past ten years because the marriages of migrants are registered in their natal parishes.

14 The records begin in 1941 because all the notary's records prior to the civil war were burned by the Republicans before the Nationalists took Vilafranca in 1939.

15 Less than 40 percent of each marriage cohort in Vilafranca made the *capitols*, principally because the town is where people without property (e.g., workers) aggregate. The percentage is probably higher for rural villages, where most adult males eventually hold a piece of property, albeit a small one.

Chapter 5. Public social organization

1 General Juan Prim (1814–70) was the hero of the Battle of Tetuán and prominent in Progressive politics in the middle 1800s. A Catalan by birth, he held in later life the titles of marquis of Castillejos and count of Reus (see Carr 1966:283).

2 The Radical party was, during the 1880s and 1890s, a small splinter party of uncertain ideology and corrupt leadership. It came to prominence when Alejandro Lerroux, a Castilian lawyer, used his demagogic talents to organize the Catalan working class in the

early 1900s against the Catalan bourgeoisie. He is generally considered to have been an agent in the pay of Madrid (Brenan 1962:261).

3 The Castilian phrase *padre del país* refers to a person who, regardless of social class, political belief, or level of education, is publicly perceived to have forged the history of the country. The term is an affectionate, but deferential, description of such a person.

4 People in Vilafranca, when asked about the class of members of any association, think in terms of the family origins of the members in question. Thus a lawyer who is the son of a sharecropper is often referred to as a peasant, because his parents are sharecroppers. Most of the members of the *Ateneu*, sons of sharecroppers, obtained jobs in Vilafranco as skilled laborers in the small businesses that emerged as a result of the local elaboration of wine and the growth of the wine trade.

5 The present road system of the *comarca* (as opposed to the national highway system) was set up by the Republican municipal government of 1931–6. In addition to road building and the establishment of local secular schools, the municipal government of Vilafranca attempted various urban reforms within the district capital. The most famous of these reforms involved burning down a count's palace in the center of town in order to create a public square. The son of the count assured me that the destruction of the house was commissioned by the municipal government and executed by local members of the CNT acting at its behest.

6 Wanda Landowska was hired by the *Sociedad la Principal* to give a harpsichord concert in 1908, which was attended, according to Sabaté i Mill (1966:6), by all of Vilafranca, although not one citizen of the *comarca* had ever before heard a harpsichord played. The bourgeois stress on culture was so strong by that time that aristocrats and workers sat side by side to marvel at the playing of Landowska.

7 Don José Zulueta, a wealthy bourgeois who lived in Barcelona, was the delegate to the Cortes from the *comarca* during this period. He represented the Partido Nacional Federal, a Republican party that favored regional rights (Mas i Perera 1932:167).

8 This particular *cacique*, Señor Lostau, was a "foreigner" from Valencia who had come to the Panadés to practice law. He had early joined the Radical party and become a bastion of the *centro's* directorate. According to a biography given by Sabaté i Mill (1966:8), Señor Lostau spent most of his time walking in the *ramblas* talking to people. Possessed of immense gifts in interpersonal relationships, he is supposed to have been a founder of the elaborate code of interpersonal conduct in café society.

9 Two noted *caciques* in Vilafranca were José and Mila Fontanels, brothers and professors of art at Vilafranca schools. They were sons of a merchant and are credited with much of the development of cultural life in Vilafranca (Mas i Perera 1932:159).

10 Women, although not excluded from the bars, participate in very restricted ways in the coalitions and have no decision-making power in the establishment of alliances. A woman's role in the bar culture is to promote friendships among families, not to create instrumental relationships among men. Her formal participation is limited to Sunday afternoon promenades, including stopovers at the bars, with her husband and children.

11 The tourist bars are, of course, also products of modernization, but of a different kind. Such bars should in no way be confused with traditional *cantinas* found in most Spanish villages and towns. For the role of tourism in Mediterranean modernization, see Schneider et al. (1972:342–3).

12 A similar point is made in a different context for Sicily by J. Schneider (1969) and P. Schneider (1969).

13 Foreign industry has penetrated the *comarca* in the form of Cinzano vermouth, Krupp cement, and Purina Chow (Hansen 1970).

14 An individual is drunk by local standards, not when he is inebriated, which is a common occurence, but when he falls down, which is a disgrace.

15 I believe most of the tales of reprisal were escapes into fantasy. I never heard of a verifiable physical confrontation between boss and employee, although I did witness a few angry resignations.

16 This observation was corroborated by photographs of these individuals taken before 1960.

17 Two of many cases I myself was involved in were the following. I was once victimized by Don Disco to the tune of 1,000 pesetas; connections were able to quash the ticket in half an hour, and I received a cheerful apology from the chief of police. Near the end of my stay in 1966, my stipend check was delayed and my funds were low. A friend, conveniently owner of a local bank, simply instructed the head of foreign exchange to issue any sum I requested. While I pride myself on having an honest face, my anthropological training suggests that an honest face without connections would have had to take up a beggar's bowl under similar circumstances.

18 Murphy's law states: "If anything can go wrong, it will."

19 I was surprised to find such high degrees of correspondence between informants in both respects. Particularly startling was the 85 percent correspondence in placing individuals in the prestige slots they had created. Their correspondence could be stretched even higher by using the results of back-up interviews concerning the fourteen to sixteen individuals who were initially controversial.

Chapter 6. The faces of power in the Alto Panadés

1 The *guardia civil*, formed in the mid 1800s as a rural political police force employed principally against Andalusian brigands, does not permit its personnel to serve in their native areas; thus no Catalans serve in Catalonia. See Brenan (1962:70) for a discussion of the history of the *guardia*. Catalans usually claim there is no such thing as a Catalan *guardia civil*; to serve in this body would be a disgrace.

2 Within twenty-four hours of occupying my quarters in a remote hamlet, the *guardia* arrived to quiz me on the nature of my business in the area.

3 Criminal insanity cases are typically those in which someone who is mentally ill goes berserk and threatens public order. There were seven or eight cases of this during my stay, all handled by the *guardia*.

4 Saint Felix, the patron saint of the Alto Panadés, is feted in May each year. Some local residents took the mayor's accident to have a religious significance.

5 Popular elections for councilmen may be held if the mayor deems it appropriate; there have been three such elections since 1939.

6 Linz and Miguel (1966:330) list the following groups as illustrating limited pluralism at the national ministerial level: Falangist, Traditionalist, various groups representing political Catholicism, the apolitical technical and civil services, and the military (further subdivided by politcal leanings). The number of such groups in the Alto Panadés is much more limited.

7 For example, the mayor's two closest friends, one a printer and the other a mortician, are frequently in the *ayuntamiento*. Also the lieutenant mayor has two close friends who are councilmen.

8 Opus Dei is a semiclandestine Catholic organization that has recently been represented in the national ministries (Linz 1962:330). It appears to be dominated by wealthy individuals with an advanced degree of social consciousness.

9 For the reason that the members of the Young Catholic Workers are under constant surveillance and endure regular harassment by the police.

10 Parish priests are quick to point out that regular communicants of the church do not exceed 10 percent of the population.

11 At 1967 prices, 60 million pesetas was equivalent to $1 million. The money was spent on constructing and equipping two large buildings to accommodate the elaboration of table wine and (at a future date) champagne.

12 An earlier cooperative generated by the same proprietors was closed to general participation. In fact, it was an exclusive club for the twenty large proprietors, and it failed because they cheated each other.

13 Many sharecroppers will not join the cooperative because they distrust the large proprietors who dominate its directorate; others will not join because they wish to be masters of their own destinies, which is a little quixotic at present.

Chapter 7. Concluding remarks

1 The fate of the Catalan bourgeoisie has many parallels in Latin America, where imperialist high finance has detoured the Latin American bourgeoisie from a developmental course. See, for example, Gunder Frank (1969) on Chile and Brazil, Borricaud (1966) on Peru, Dean (1970) on São Paulo, and R. Hansen (1971) on Mexico.

BIBLIOGRAPHY

Anon. 1966. *Ponencia de Población*, Organización Sindical, Vilafranca del Panadés.

Arensberg, C., and Kimball, S. 1940. *Family and Community in Ireland*, Cambridge University Press, Cambridge.

Barnes, J. A. 1968. "Networks and Politcal Processes." In M. Swartz, ed., *Local Level Politics*, Aldine, Chicago, 107–30.

Barth, F. 1966. "Models of Social Organization." *Royal Anthropological Institute, Occasional Paper* 23:1–33.

Benach y Sonet, P. 1911. *En defensa de la rabassa morta*, Arturo Suarez, Barcelona.

Bendix, R. 1967. "Tradition and Modernity Reconsidered." *Comparative Studies in Society and History* 9:292–347.

Bloch, M. 1966. *Feudal Society*, 2 vols. University of Chicago Press, Chicago.

Blok, A. 1969. "Mafia and peasant rebellion as contrasting factors in Sicilian Latifundism." *Archives Europeennes de Sociologie* 10:95–116.

Borricaud, F. 1970. *Power and Society in Contemporary Peru*, Praeger, New York.

Braudel, F. 1946. "Monnaies et civilizations: de l'or du Soudan à l'argent d'Amérique." *Annales* (ESC) 1 (1):9–22.

Brenan, G. 1962. *The Spanish Labyrinth*, Cambridge University Press, New York.

Campllonch, I. 1917. *Cellers cooperatius de producció i venda*, Fidel Giró, Barcelona.

Carr, R. 1966. *Spain, 1808–1939*, Clarendon Press, Oxford.

Dahrendorf, R. 1959. *Class and Class Conflict in Industrial Society*, Stanford University Press, Stanford, Calif.

Dean, W. 1969. *The Industrialization of São Paulo 1880–1945*, University of Texas Press, Austin.

Dore, R. P. 1969. "Making Sense of History." *European Journal of Sociology* 10:295–305.

Elliot, J. H. 1963a. *The Revolt of the Catalans, 1599–1640*, Cambridge University Press, London.

1963b. *Imperial Spain*, St. Martin's Press, New York.

Erikson, K. 1970. "Labor in the Politcal Process of Brazil: Corporativism in a Modernizing Nation." Doctoral dissertation, Columbia University.

Fuentes, C. 1969. "Viva Zapata." *New York Review of Books*, March 13:5–11.

Garcia Vénero, M. 1953. *Cambó*, Imprènta Suarez, Madrid.

Giralt i Raventós, E. 1952. "La viticultura y el comercio catalán del siglo XVIII." *Estudios de historia moderna* 2:159–76.

1958. "En torno al precio del trigo en Barcelona durante el siglo XVI." *Hispania* 18:38–61.

1964. "El conflicto *rabassaire* y la cuestión agraria en Cataluña hasta 1936." *Revista del trabajo* 7(3):51–72.

1966. "El passat de l'economía del Pénedès." *Coloquio comarcal sobre economia del Pénedès*, Artes Gráficas, Vilafranca del Panadés, 5–24.

Giró, P. 1966. *Ponencia agricultura, riqueza forestal y ganadería*, Concejo de Trabajo, Vilafranca del Panadés.

Gunder Frank, A. 1969. *Capitalism and Underdevelopment in Latin America*, Modern Reader, New York.

Hansen, E. 1969. "The State and Land Tenure Conflict in Rural Catalonia, Spain." *Anthropological Quarterly* 42(3):214–43.

———. 1970. "Political Dimensions of Social Change in Rural Catalonia." Doctoral dissertation, University of Michigan.

———. 1974. "Contrasting Styles of Urbanization in Rural Catalonia." *Annals, New York Academy of Sciences* 220(6):509–21.

Hansen, R. 1971. *The Politics of Mexican Development*, Johns Hopkins Press, Baltimore.

Hinojosa, E. 1918. *El régimen señorial y la cuestión agraria en Cataluña*, Fernandez Guerra, Madrid.

Lasswell, H. 1963. *Politics: Who Gets What, When and How*, Meridian Books, New York.

Leeds, A. 1964. "Brazilian Careers and Social Structure." *American Anthropologist* 66:1321–47.

Lenin, V. I. 1952. "The State and Revolution." In *Selected Works*, vol. 2, part 1, Foreign Languages Publishing House, Moscow, 199–325.

Linz, J. 1962. "An Authoritarian Regime: Spain." In E. Allardt and Y. Littunen, eds. *Parties, Cleavages, and Ideologies*, Transactions of the Westermark Society, Helsinki, 291–341.

———. 1970. Early State-building and Late Peripheral Nationalisms Against the State: The Case of Spain. UNESCO, Paris, 4–5.

Linz, J., and Miguel, A. 1966. "Within Nation Differences and Comparisons: The Eight Spains." In S. Rokkan and R. Merritt, eds. *Comparing Nations*, Yale University Press, New Haven, Conn., 267–319.

Lipset, S. 1968. "Values, Education and Entreprenuership." In S. Lipset and A. Solari, eds. *Elites in Latin America*, Oxford University Press, New York, 3–60.

Marx, K., and Engels, F. 1955. *Selected Works*, 2 vols., Foreign Language Publishing House, Moscow.

Mas i Perera, P. 1932. *Vilafranca del Pénedès*, Editorial Barcino, Barcelona.

Maspons i Anglasells, F. 1935. *La llei de la familia*, Editorial Barcino; Barcelona.

Merriman, R. B. 1936. *The Rise and Fall of the Spanish Empire*, vol. 3., Oxford University Press, New York.

Mestre Artigas, C. 1961. *Manuel Raventós Domenech*, Artes Gráficas, Vilafranca del Panadés.

Moore, B. 1966. *Social Origins of Dictatorship and Democracy*, Beacon Press, Boston.

Nun, J. 1968. "A Latin American Phenonomenon. The Middle Class Military Coup." In Petras, J. and Zeitlin, M., eds. *Latin America: Reform or Revoultion?* Fawcett, New York, 145–85.

Ortega y Gasset, J. 1937. *Invertebrate Spain*, Norton, New York.

Payne, S. 1967a. *Politics and the Military in Modern Spain*, Stanford University Press, Stanford, Calif.

———. 1967b. *Franco's Spain*, Crowell Press, New York.

Rostow, W. 1961. *The Stages of Economic Growth*, M.I.T. Press, Boston.

Sabaté i Mill, A. 1966. "El Casino de la Unión." In *Centenario del Casino, 1853–1966*, Vilafranca del Panadés, 8 pp.

Schmitter, P. 1971. *Interest, Conflict, and Political Change in Brazil*, Stanford University Press, Stanford, Calif.

Schneider, J. 1969. "Family Patrimonies and Economic Behaviour in Western Sicily." *Anthropological Quarterly* 42:109–29.

Schneider, P. 1969. "Honor and Conflict in a Sicilian Town." *Anthropological Quarterly* 42:130–54.

Schneider, P., Schneider, J., and Hansen E. 1972. "Modernization and Development: The Role of Regional Elites and Noncorporate Groups in the European Mediterranean." *Comparative Studies in Society and History* 14:328–50.

Schneider, R. 1971. *The Political System of Brazil*, Columbia University Press, New York.

Silverman, S. 1966. "An Ethnographic Approach to Social Stratification: Prestige in a Central Italian Community." *American Anthropologist* 68:899–921.

Stancliffe, M. 1966. Cultural and Ecological Aspects of Marriage, Succession and Migration in a Peasant Community of the Catalan Pyrenees." Doctoral dissertation, Columbia University.

Stavenhagen, R. 1967. "Las relaciones entre la estratificación social y la dinámica de clases." In A. Leeds, ed. *Social Structures, Stratification and Mobility*, Pan American Union Studies and Monographs, vol. 7:126–51.

Tamames, R. 1965. *Estructura económica de España*, 3rd ed., Sociedad de Estudios y Publicaciones, Madrid.

1970. *Introducción a la economía española*, Alianza Editorial, Madrid.

Trotsky, L. 1937. *The History of the Russian Revolution*, Gollancz, London.

Trueta, R. J. 1946. *The Spirit of Catalonia*, Oxford University Press, London.

Vicens Vives, J. 1959. *Cataluña en el siglo XIX*, Ediciones Rialp, Barcelona.

1969. *An Economic History of Spain*, Princeton University Press, Princeton, N.J.

Vidal Barraguer, J. M. 1966. "El futur de l'agricultura comarcal." *Coloquio sobre economía del Panadés*, Artes Gráficas, Vilafranca del Panadés, 27–46.

Vilar, P. 1956. "Le temps du 'quichotte.'" *Europe*, January:3–16.

1962. *Catalogne dans l'Espagne moderne*, 3 vols. S.E.V.P.E.N., Paris.

Wallerstein, I. 1974a. *The Modern World System: Capitalist Agriculture and the European World Economy*, Academic Press, New York.

1974b. "The Rise and Future Demise of the World Capitalist System: Concepts for Comparative Analysis." *Comparative Studies in Society and History* 16(4):387–415.

Wolf, E. 1959. *Sons of the Shaking Earth*, University of Chicago Press, Chicago.

1966. "Kinship, Friendship, and Patron-Client Relationships." In M. Banton, ed., *The Social Anthropology of Complex Societies*. Tavistock, London, 1–22.

Wolf, E. R., and Hansen, E. 1967. "Caudillo Politics: A Structural Analysis." *Comparative Studies in Society and History* 9:167–78.

INDEX

179